a GRAIN OF TRUTH

HOW POLLEN BROUGHT A MURDERER TO JUSTICE

LYNNE MILNE

First published in Australia in 2005 by
Reed New Holland
an imprint of New Holland Publishers (Australia) Pty Ltd
Sydney • Auckland • London • Cape Town
14 Aquatic Drive Frenchs Forest NSW 2086 Australia
218 Lake Road Northcote Auckland New Zealand
86 Edgware Road London W2 2EA United Kingdom
80 McKenzie Street Cape Town 8001 South Africa

National Library of Australia Cataloguing-in-Publication Data:

Milne, Lynne.
A grain of truth.

Bibliography.
ISBN 1 877069 02 7.

1. Forensic botany - Queensland. 2. Palynology - Queensland. I. Title.

363.2509943

Publisher: Louise Egerton
Project Editor: Yani Silvana
Cover design: saso content and design
Cover photo: Karen Moskowitz/gettyimages
Production: Grace Gutwein
Printer: Griffin Press

Note: Minor details of the case and the names and personalities of some of the people in this book have been altered to protect their identity.

Acknowledgements

My publisher, Louise Egerton, who conceptualised this book, persuaded me to write it and guided me through the initial process, and my editor, Yani Silvana, who pulled it all together, deserve medals for their critical editing and for suffering my tardiness in meeting deadlines and propensity to cause them grief. My gratitude to Lyn and Malcolm Hall for sharing Sam and their story with me is immeasurable. Their courage, love and friendship has sustained me through tears to laughter and enriched my life. Thanks and appreciation are due to my police 'partners in crime'—Paul Zohn, Brad Hall and John Leembruggen—for providing additional case information and editing relevant passages, and Paul Stewart, Haydn Green and Mark Reynolds for their assistance and advice; the Queensland Office of the Director of Public Prosecutions for transcripts of the committal hearing; David Haig for laboratory photographs; Glen Gloster and John Hall for information on the revegetation of Noosa Spit (Noosa Woods) and Noosa wattles; Judith Fordham, Ian Dadour, Les Pedley and Bruce Maslin for 'expert' advice so that I may 'get it almost right'; Miira Gallegos for critically reading the first draft and help with two figures; and my fellow forensic palynologists Dallas Mildenhall, Patricia Wiltshire and Vaughn Bryant for their casework over the years, their friendship and advice. A multitude of hugs and thanks to my family, friends and colleagues who have encouraged and supported me throughout the period this book covers and while it was being written. And above all—Sam.

For Michael and Corey

To all parents: give your kids loads of hugs and cuddles, because you will have those to remember.

Lyn Hall, 1996, in a television interview after the murder of her daughter, Samantha

Contents

In the Beginning

Thankfully my car knew its way home along Kenmore Road, which winds through the back of the western suburbs of Brisbane, high above the river it follows. Lined with magnificent gum trees and tropical gardens that belie the presence of houses, this drive to and from the University of Queensland was my twice-daily treat. But on that Sunday morning I didn't even notice it. Although my arms and torso were locked into the rhythm of negotiating the bends, as though I were riding a familiar rollercoaster, my thoughts were on the parklands of Noosa, another beautiful place in southern Queensland that, in the past few years, had been a silent witness to murder. The killers of a young girl accosted while innocently riding her bike through a park in the late 1980s had been brought to justice. But still at large was the person who murdered a young mother in 1996. It was now early 1997, and several days previously I had been approached to work on this most recent Noosa homicide.

Until that day, the idea of applying my skills and knowledge of pollen morphology (structure) to help solve crimes had not crossed my mind. Several of my international colleagues had done so successfully, but it was not a career path I had considered. The magnitude of this request and the responsibility that working on the case would carry were competing with thoughts of my two young daughters' suspicions that my doctoral project on pollen morphology was not going to be 'useful to people'.

Some six years previously my eldest daughter's grade 3 teacher had summoned me to the school for a meeting. Belinda is a delightful free spirit. Somewhat brighter than average, she had a tendency to become bored in class, directing her extra energy towards activities not in the curriculum. Expecting to be dealing with this aspect of her behaviour I was stunned to learn that her teacher, Mrs Shaw, thought she was living in a fantasy world. She was telling strange stories about her family.

I sat there frozen. Belinda was not a good liar. She didn't like fantasy stories and her favourite books were *Nick the Sea Captain* and *Tell Me Why*. My thoughts raced through some of the not so normal things about our family. Her dad could burp and say Bulawayo at the same time. He'd also been cautioned by police for running out to collect the morning paper in his birthday suit, and writing rude messages on our garbage bin. The previous two bins had been stolen in as many weeks. Maybe Belinda was spreading the message that her little sister, Caroline, was an alien—a not uncommon comment at home when they had a disagreement. I braced myself for some awful 'home' truths.

'She says her dad is blind in one eye because he was hit by a beach umbrella', challenged Mrs Shaw.

'Yes, that's right', I said in measured tones, fearing that the next allegation might not be so easy to explain. After offering embarrassed condolences, Mrs Shaw continued.

'She says you have cancer.'

'Yes, that's right.' In fact I was in the late stages of preparation for radioactive iodine therapy, which meant I was off my medication and only able to walk about ten steps at a time. On the long walk to her classroom Belinda had to encourage me to take each step, and was as excited as a mother watching her baby take its first steps when I'd managed 16 steps one after the other. The tables were turning. I was beginning to relax and Mrs Shaw was squirming with embarrassment. She apologetically broached the next of Belinda's 'fantasies'.

'She says you are doing a PhD.'

'Yes, that's right.' Phew, our family had survived without any awkward revelations.

The next day Mrs Shaw sent Belinda home with a sticker for me to put on my microscope, my tool of trade. It had a wise owl on it and bore the message 'You are a star'.

In grade 3 Belinda was eight years old and she thought the sticker was very appropriate. She was proud that I had a degree in geology just like her dad, and many of her friends' dads. She was especially proud that I was working towards my PhD. But towards the end of her primary school years she began to question how the research I was conducting on pollen was going to be beneficial to the community at large.

Palynology, the study of pollen, spores and other microscopic plant bodies, has numerous applications that are important to our modern way of life. Commercially, it is employed to date rocks encountered during exploration drilling for minerals, water and petroleum. One of its earliest and continuing uses is helping to unravel the history of plant life on our planet. Convincing a 12-year-old that investigating the evolutionary history of a small group of Australian plants was going to be 'useful' was difficult. It was even harder for her to convey this information to her schoolmates. Her peers had student mothers doing something they could relate to, like training to be teachers or studying environmental science.

'Mummy, Sarah's mum is doing a PhD on cancer. What you're doing isn't very useful, is it?' Such comments were becoming increasingly common. It was the quizzically raised eyebrows and meaningful and lingering looks suggesting that I should get my act together that I had no concrete answers for. Pure scientific research and serendipity have combined to form the basis of many of the world's most important discoveries. So all I could say was that 'something useful will come up one day'. Was this the useful thing? Could I help solve a murder?

At this stage I knew only the barest of details about the case I had been asked to work on. The body of a woman had been found in bushland at Noosa Heads, some two hours' drive north of Brisbane, in August 1996. The victim had lived in nearby Gympie.

It was almost eight months since the victim's body had been found. In the back of my mind was a comment one of my Australian colleagues had made, that the handling of forensic samples prior to a palynologist receiving them has often compromised the outcome of pollen analysis. In other words, because most police are unfamiliar with palynology as an investigative tool, soil samples and items upon which pollen analysis is to be conducted can be contaminated or damaged if they're not collected and stored correctly. Similarly, airborne pollen and pollen from the hands and clothing of other forensic scientists (e.g. pathologists and soil and fibre experts) who first examine the samples may be mixed with pollen from the crime scene. This means that a palynologist might spend a lot of time working on a case only to find that because the samples were not handled correctly the evidence is not accepted by the court. My colleague therefore summarily refused any police requests to help them with investigations. I wasn't going to be so hasty, but I did need to learn more about the case before making a commitment to work on it.

Aside from deciding whether the samples had been handled and stored correctly, I also needed to examine both the personal and professional pros and cons of being involved in a criminal investigation. If my evidence was successful in helping to arrest and convict a murderer, I would certainly be very 'useful' in my children's eyes. They could join the bragging brigade at school. On the other hand, this was a tenuous reason for taking on such a responsibility and should not sway my decision.

Personally, I had to consider the time and money involved. My PhD thesis was officially due to be finished by the end of June and I was already two months behind schedule. I would need an extension anyway. But even then, could I spare the time? Would it compromise the outcome of my project? Having been a sole parent and also a student for the past four years, neither money nor time was plentiful. To make ends meet, I worked part-time as an electron microscopist for the Department of Earth Sciences at the University of Queensland. This Sunday morning drive along Kenmore Road was not a joy ride, visit to church, or any other kind of Sunday outing. I was heading home. While the children slept I made up the weekly hours I was committed to by working from 6.00 am until 10.00 am every Sunday morning.

The initial approach to work on the case had come from a fellow student who was already involved. Then the police had contacted me. Could I tell the difference between pollen from one plant species and that of another closely related species? From a professional point of view my answer to this was quite simple. All things being equal...yes, in most instances, I can. But do I really want to become involved in a crime investigation, especially one that has the potential to send someone to prison for much of their life? It would be a huge responsibility, but one I could cope with if there were other lines of evidence that supported mine. Am I prepared to go to court? Could be interesting, and I have no problems standing in front of a crowd and talking about something I believe in. Am I prepared to risk retribution from someone whose life I might alter dramatically? Police do that all the time. I'll get a silent phone number!

My work that morning had been routine, involving setting up a machine to slice up small pieces of coal with a diamond knife for study purposes. Once the machine was adjusted to cut the coal regularly, there was little to do but sit and watch it for ten minutes until enough sections had been cut. Even adjusting the machine was mindless, leaving plenty of time to ponder these questions.

By the time I left for home I was leaning towards agreeing to work on the murder case. But first I would need to talk to my daughters, Caroline and Belinda, then aged 12 and 15 respectively, about how they would feel if I were to be involved in a murder investigation, and be sure that they had no apprehensions. This resolved, I would need to learn more about the case so far.

The decision my daughters and I made that day was to shape my career in the following years, whether I liked it or not. Forensic science has a life of its own. Work on one case and you're on the merry-go-round. Today, eight years later in 2005, more cases, teaching police and postgraduate students, community club and society presentations and the ever-present media interest take up much of my working life. So much for an academic career in geological and botanical palynology. How times change—and how experience changes one's perspective. Police are no longer the bad guys who catch me for speeding, but people I have the utmost respect for and to whom those who commit crimes are known as 'baddies'.

Yes, police have their own lingo. For example, dogs are not four-legged furry friends—they are surveillance police. I know what evidence tape and exhibit bags are and enjoy crossing the police barriers that keep the public and media from crime scenes, while the media hang out on the other side. Ha! Wouldn't you like to know what I know! On the flip side, noisy media helicopters trying to get a sneak peek fray my nerves, and the thought of achieving a positive result in a bikie gang case gives me the creeps.

Aside from the satisfaction of the practical applications of forensic palynology, there are social bonuses. As a result of my being on the community talk circuit, my wine cellar and collection of elegant writing implements are growing, and the graveyard for potted flowering plants I am given to kill with lack of water is expanding.

Despite these varied forensic activities I have had little involvement with the human side of forensic science. Usually, the only visual contact I have with people involved in crime is with the accused while I'm in the witness box. The victims of crime are mere names on a piece of paper I sign when taking possession of forensic samples for pollen analysis. Even when attending a crime scene I feel detached from the actual crime. In Western Australia I am not called to a crime scene when a body, living victims, or the relatives of a victim are there. This is the domain of police forensic experts, and forensic pathologists and entomologists. I may arrive at a scene a few hours after the crime happened and a pool of blood may still be there...but apart from the odd twinge of sadness when it occurs to me that this is the blood of someone's mother, father or child, and that the house I am at was a functioning home the day before, I give little thought to the actual crime and the effect it has had on the lives of people involved. Hard-hearted? No, I'm just involved in doing my job—which doesn't involve people or emotions.

This detachment is not a bad way for forensic scientists to approach their work because it helps ensure impartiality. They don't set out to find a suspect guilty, or prove their innocence. They just present their scientific findings.

Police are somewhat different. The majority of my contact with police is through teaching, attending forensic seminars and social events, collecting and returning forensic samples, and discussing my results with them on the phone or in person. At these times they are a culture on their own. They joke a lot, have affectionate nicknames for their colleagues, and are generally great fun to be around. With this in mind it is difficult to reconcile the police I meet on such occasions with the police I meet at crime scenes. They are the same people I laughed with last week, but they are different.

Police at crime scenes rarely joke, and if they do it is apologetically, to break the tension. There is a hush in the air and they speak in serious and respectfully quiet tones. Their job involves people.

Leaving a crime scene I have often questioned my lack of emotion, wondering if there is something wrong with me because I'm not moved to tears by the reality of the situation. However, recently I discovered the reason for my lack of emotion—I had never met any victims of crime. My perspective changed radically when, years after I had been involved in the Noosa case which began my career as a forensic palynologist, I met the family of the young mother who was murdered.

Samantha

After completing my PhD in late 1997, the girls and I moved to Perth, my home town. Six years later, in August 2003, I returned to Queensland to learn more about the Noosa murder case with a view to including it in a book about forensic palynology. Although I was familiar with the scientific aspects of the case, I knew little of the police investigation and nothing about the victim, her family and the person convicted of her murder—except for photos of the victim in newspaper articles and one of the suspect, handcuffed to a detective, after he'd been arrested.

I had arranged to travel to Maroochydore to meet with Paul Zohn, one of the arresting officers I had worked with on the case, and then go on to Noosa. Meeting with Paul was to be the starting point of my research. Aside from being able to provide me with details of the early part of the investigation, he was my link to the victim's family. Not that I personally wanted to intrude on the lives of these people, but I hoped Paul would let them know that I wanted to use the case in my book—without their blessing I wouldn't have felt comfortable using it.

The early morning traffic was worse than I'd remembered, so I phoned Paul to let him know I was running late. But he was ill, and cancelled the meeting. I was devastated. It was Friday and I was due in Sydney on Sunday and back in Perth on Wednesday. On the spur of the moment I agreed to meet him on Wednesday and worry about reorganising my schedule later.

My plans for the day dashed, I went to Noosa anyway and visited the site where the victim's body had been found. It had changed markedly in seven years. Gone were the masses of juvenile wattle plants that had grown in the bushland. In their place a small cross stood in a clearing surrounded by weeds (Plate 1). Gone too, was the solid bank of wattle bushes that had leant over the side of the parking bay in which the murderer had allegedly parked. The only evidence of wattles here now was a small flowering bush peeping out from the greenery beside the car park (Plate 2).

The small cross that marked the spot near where the body had been found, and the simple poignant inscription on its plaque, were my first encounter with the human side of a crime I had helped to resolve. The emotional impact this had on me caught me by surprise. In a daze I wandered through the nearby bushland for an hour or so, taking photographs and pondering my unexpected reaction. Later, while booking into a hotel for the night, I impulsively asked for directions to the road to Gympie, where the dead woman had lived.

After settling into my room, and with several hours to fill before nightfall, something compelled me to drive out of town along the road from Noosa to Gympie, the same road that the murderer had driven along with the body of his victim strapped into the front seat of the car.

I had no plan of action when I left Noosa, just a strange urge to drive down that road. Experience has taught me that following such urges sometimes leads to something important. Bookstores are the worst. Sometimes as I hurriedly walk past them they draw me in. Irritated, I follow the pull and walk briskly up and down the aisles to prove my muse wrong for once. But no, that pull again, and I must stop, turn, and look at a shelf—and there it is, the first title in view is something I need to learn from at that time, or the perfect gift for a birthday. Damn, it was right again.

Was my magical muse at work again? What was I to achieve by driving towards this town? The luxury of a dusk dinner in an outdoor café in Noosa was beckoning me and I didn't envisage driving all the way to Gympie and back, so I decided to drive until it felt right to turn around.

As I drove towards the victim's home town, questions about the case flooded my mind. How was she killed? Why did the killer, after murdering her in Gympie, drive her body to central Noosa? Did he plan this? Dense rainforest lined much of the road, and at each new bend there seemed to be a better place to dispose of a body than in a popular tourist destination.

These questions and musings so preoccupied me that before I knew it I was on the outskirts of Gympie. What now? Perhaps I should look for places mentioned in the police statement of another expert witness who worked on the case. I had a copy of his statement with me.

Having no map of Gympie, I accidentally veered away from the town centre and onto the scenic drive, where I chanced upon a sign for the Mt

Pleasant Hotel. What luck! It was mentioned in the statement. I stopped at this quaint old pub to ask for directions, but I got more than I bargained for. Dave, the man in the bottle shop, had known the victim well and gave me a phone number to follow up.

Dave's directions were good, but Gympie was larger than I had imagined, and I got lost. I stared at the number on the small piece of paper in my hand. Picking up my mobile phone I looked at it expectantly, hoping it would tell me what to do. But it was mute and I didn't feel brave enough to dial the number. That I had the number was miraculous in itself. I would pluck up the courage to use it when I returned to Perth. It was time to find my way back to Noosa. I put the phone down on the passenger seat, started the rented car, and was nosing it out of the parking bay to return the way I had come when my phone came to life.

'I've just talked to them. They would love to meet you. Can you drive out there now?' the voice on the phone asked. It was Dave from the bottle shop. I was stunned, speechless, and it seemed a whole minute passed before I could answer.

'Is it very far away?' I asked tentatively.

'It's a bit of a way along a dirt road, but they said if you phone them they'll give you directions. Give them a call now and drop by the bottle shop on your way and we'll look at a map', he said.

Hastily, before I could lose my nerve, I looked at the piece of paper, took a deep breath, and dialled the number.

'Hello, it's Lynne Milne speaking. Dave suggested I call you.' It wasn't so hard after all. The woman's voice was welcoming. She was looking forward to meeting me. My throat tightened as I took down the directions to their farm. She said it would be quite a drive, much of it on dirt road, and that it would almost be dark by the time I arrived.

The car found its way back to the bottle shop and Dave and I pored over a map to see which would be the best way out of town.

'Do they drink?' I asked.

'Yes', Dave said.

'What do they drink?'

'He brews his own.'

'Just beer, or does he make his own wine too?' I queried.

'No, not wine, but he makes almost everything else', Dave replied.

I began to relax. My dad and my former husband brewed their own beer and I'd been a willing helper in the making and the drinking. I would have something in common with these people.

'What about a bottle of liqueur?'

'He makes that, too', Dave replied with a grin.

I'd been looking forward to a quiet glass of wine with dinner in a sidewalk café in Noosa—and felt like one right then.

'Do you think they would mind if I took some wine out?'

'No. I'm sure they'll help you drink it', Dave assured me.

So there I was, bottle of wine on the front seat of the car, driving along a dusty country road where the sparsely dotted houses and their identifying numbers were hidden by trees. Driving along dirt roads is usually fun, but this time it was tricky. The sun was sinking fast, and shadows from the dense vegetation were cast right across the small country road, forming mesmerising stripes. I struggled to see and breathe, not through the dust that still hung in the air from the car that must have gone before me, but through my brimming eyes and the emotion tightening my throat. This well of emotion threatening to overcome me was a surprise. It came out of nowhere—some hidden place that had never been tapped before. Although I was driving to meet people I didn't know and hadn't expected to meet, it felt as if I was going home.

Must pull myself together—don't want to end up in the ditch at the side of the road or arrive with a tear-streaked face. My mind was racing as I clenched the steering wheel. What must they be thinking? Will they resent my intrusion into their lives? The dam of my lower eyelid broached and tears flowed down my cheeks as the thought of what they must have suffered overwhelmed me. Now I understood. This is why police are not their jovial selves at crime scenes.

Finding the street number I was looking for was a challenge. Had I driven past it? No, a little further to go. It must be just around the corner.

Two dogs came racing out to greet me as I drove into the farm yard. Their owners, a retired couple dressed in their farm work clothes and boots, followed close behind and warned them off. Unwinding stiff fingers from the steering wheel I opened the car door and reached out for the warm handshake that the man with kindly eyes offered. She followed, her wonderfully untamed long wavy hair haloed in the early dusk light. The lump in my throat grew as she walked towards me with a welcoming smile. I needed to hug her—and I did, the warmth of this stranger relieving my anxiety and confirming that this was the destination I had unknowingly sought.

No, I had no trouble finding their place, and no, I didn't mind going with them to herd the cows into the night enclosure before we went inside. The woman and I stood making small talk while her husband took the dogs back into the farmhouse compound. As he returned, a boy in his early teens came bounding towards us to discuss the order in which his evening chores were to be done. They bantered and joked as only those who have great love for each other do, and his eyes sparkled with a cheekiness from a face that was hauntingly familiar. She watched him lope across the road to tend to his cattle, and murmured, 'My daughter's son'.

Samantha Jane Hall came into the world on 23 December 1967 in a small farmhouse near the English village of Tideswell. On a rainy day in August 1970 a two and half year old Sam, as she was affectionately called by her family, arrived in Australia with her English parents and older brother and sister. They settled in Adelaide, South Australia. Sam was a gentle, happy and bouncy child. She grew into an attractive young woman, a free spirit, beautiful on the outside and beautiful on the inside, as her mother would later describe her (Plate 3). Even as a young teenager, employers recognised her outgoing nature and compassionate warmth as an asset in customer service. She met everyone on an equal basis, seeing the person behind the face, but she detested cruelty of any kind.

In 1983, when she was 16 years old, Sam moved out of the family home to be closer to her workplace. Her housemate was friendly with the brother of a young man, Reas Holden, who was in prison. Few people had visited Reas during his term in prison, so his brother had asked Sam's housemate to visit him. She did, and she took Sam with her.

Sam knew of Reas. They had grown up in the same neighbourhood and attended the same primary and secondary schools. He was five years older than her, the same age as her brother, and had been in and out of institutions and prison from a young age for petty crime including car theft, robbery and robbery with violence. He had married in his late teens and was now estranged from his wife. Sam felt sorry for him. She felt she could 'fix' him and keep him out of prison. Helping people less fortunate than herself was one of Sam's endearing traits. She often borrowed money from her parents to help friends in need, then paid her family back even if her friends hadn't repaid her. People who needed 'fixing' were drawn to her, and she willingly embraced their cause. Reas Holden was the ultimate challenge.

After her first visit to Reas in prison Sam wrote to him and visited him whenever she could arrange transport to do so. By the time Reas was released from prison their friendship had developed into a more serious relationship. Although alarmed at their younger daughter's blossoming romance with a convicted criminal, Sam's parents had little choice but to embrace the relationship or risk alienating her. She was in love.

In time Sam's family came to know Reas well. He was polite and considerate around them and prepared to help out at short notice. A phone call and he would be there. Reas and Sam's relationship had its highs and lows, but to Sam's parents' relief her influence did keep Reas out of prison and the union appeared to be a happy one.

While visiting Queensland for their son's wedding shortly after Sam and Reas became an item, Sam's parents fell in love with the southern Queensland climate. Five years later, in 1988, they sold up the family home in Adelaide, bought a small farm near their son's home, and settled down to a quiet retirement. Moving interstate away from their daughters was a wrench, but it was time to make a life of their own. Their eldest daughter was married with a family and Sam, at almost 21, had been in a stable and happy relationship for almost five years. She and Reas had been trying to start a family, but without success, and had discussed getting married some time in the future.

Shortly after her parents moved to Queensland Sam began fertility treatment. In December 1989 their first son was born, and two years later they were blessed with another son. Sam's parents were delighted that at last she had the family she had longed for.

This illusion of a happy family unit was not to last for long. During a heated argument Reas pulled a gun on Sam and the children and threatened to kill them. Sam went into hiding and her sister gathered up the small boys, aged five months and two and a half years, and flew with them to Queensland. She dropped them at her parents' place and flew back to Adelaide the same day. Sam remained in hiding for several months. Despite her fear of Reas, Sam continued to love him and they eventually reunited on the condition that, although they would live together, he would sign full custody of the children over to her.

Two years later Sam's parents received an urgent phone call from their eldest daughter. Sam was ill, and the doctor had advised that she needed rest. Her mother flew to Adelaide to be with her and help care for the children. On arrival, she found that Sam was disturbed and frightened. The doctor couldn't provide a definite diagnosis for Sam's apparent ill health. Was she ill with fear?

When they were alone Sam told her mother that lights had been going on and off inside the house or flashing from across the road, and that she'd heard footsteps on the roof. Were these figments of her imagination? She thought not. She believed it was Reas trying to unnerve her. Was he trying to kill her or have her declared mentally unfit so that he could have sole custody of the children?

Sam's mother was disturbed by her daughter's frame of mind, but she too witnessed lights apparently turning on and off by themselves, and heard noises on the roof when she and Sam were alone in the house. Despite Reas appearing to be supportive of Sam, her mother was uneasy. Something was amiss. There was an unpleasant undercurrent in the young couple's relationship and there was something they weren't telling her.

On the doctor's advice Sam's mother took the two boys back to Queensland with her to give Sam time to recover and sort out her relationship with Reas. Some serious talking must have gone on between the young couple when they were left alone, because six weeks later they drove to Queensland, arriving at Sam's parents' farm on Christmas Eve, 1994. They wanted to start afresh. For three weeks they stayed with Sam's parents while looking for a house to rent in the nearby town. During that time Sam was quick to anger, but Reas was controlled and his genial self—with one exception. During a raging row, and in front of Sam's parents, he threatened to kill her one day.

Sam, Reas and their two sons settled in the town of Gympie, a short drive from Sam's parents' farm. The grandparents enjoyed being close to their daughter and grandsons, and Reas was happy to help on their farm in his spare time. This closeness also gave Sam's family an insight into her relationship with Reas. What they saw was disturbing and they became increasingly worried for her safety. A large bruise on Sam's breast alerted them to the fact that physical abuse was a regular occurrence in her relationship, not the occasional happening they had believed. Reas was also a philanderer, and Sam told her mother she always knew when he was 'at it again' because his violence towards her increased.

Her concerned parents encouraged Sam to leave Reas, but Sam was hesitant. She still loved Reas, but she didn't want her boys to grow up to be 'women-beaters'. On the other hand, she believed that if she were to leave Reas he would find her and kill her. He had said he would do just that so often. The prospect of leaving the boys motherless didn't daunt him—he would kill them too, and himself, and then they would all be a happy family together in the hereafter.

Instead of leaving Reas, Sam set about making the family home unwelcoming so that he would choose to leave her of his own accord. She adopted an attitude of silent indifference. Reas finally moved out about May 1996.

With Reas gone Sam felt free to reveal to her parents the cause of her mysterious illness in Adelaide. She explained that Reas had been encouraging her to use amphetamines, and that she had become dependent on him to supply them—a situation he seemed to welcome. On that particular occasion she believed he'd spiked her coffee with morphine, a drug that she reacted badly to, so that it would appear she had overdosed. When she and Reas moved to

Queensland she had gone off the drugs 'cold turkey' which explained why she had been quick to anger when they first arrived.

Sam's boys, now aged four and six, were in the habit of spending Friday nights and Saturdays on her parents' property. With the dogs, chickens and cows, it was a small child's wonderland. But late on Thursday 29 August that year, Reas asked Sam if he could have the children for the weekend. They would stay with his parents, who had moved to Gympie several years beforehand and were renting a small property on the outskirts of town. Sam agreed. How could she refuse? He had never before asked to have the boys for the whole weekend.

Worried at this turn-about in attitude Sam tried to rationalise Reas' motive. He had seen more of the children in the previous week than usual because the hot water system where he lived had broken down, and he needed to shower. Sam was prepared to let him into her home to use the bathroom while the boys were there, but not when she was alone. Perhaps he had enjoyed those short visits.

Sam slept fitfully that Thursday night, thankful that her mother had agreed to phone her early in the morning. Friday would be a long day. She wanted to get an early start because she was going on a full-day kindergarten excursion with her younger son, and Reas' mother, a stickler for punctuality, was to join them.

At 6.45 am on Friday Sam answered her mother's wake-up call. Yes, she was up and almost ready to go. They chatted happily about the activities planned for the day. Mention of Reas' mother reminded Sam to tell her mother that the boys would not be going to the farm that night. Her mother was startled and concerned when she learnt that Reas wanted to have them for the whole weekend—this was out of character and outside their normal agreement. Driving with Reas, who had a habit of taking corners on two wheels, frightened his small sons to tears. Sam had tried to limit the time they spent with him in his car.

Admitting to her mother that she also felt uncomfortable about it, Sam cut the conversation short. It was making her more paranoid than she already was. This was the last time Sam's mother would speak to her.

After arriving back in Gympie from the day out, Sam drove her younger son and Reas' mother to the house where they would spend the weekend. Reas had already collected their elder son from school. On the way home Sam stopped at the Mt Pleasant Hotel, where she held a part-time job. She had one drink to celebrate the end of a hectic day and left at 5.30 pm, promising to be back later that evening after showering and changing her clothes.

Although she was tired from the day's activities, Sam was looking forward to her regular Friday night drinks with friends. She was also looking forward to seeing Matt, the new man in her life, who she had been dating for six weeks. He would be working for part of the evening behind the bar or in the bottle shop, but would be free to join them during his dinner break. Matt was genuine and down-to-earth and he treated her well. It was a novelty for Sam, and a relief, to be in a relationship free of uncertainty and fear.

Samantha Hall was a creature of habit. After showering and washing her hair she wrapped a towel around her body and put another towel, turban style, around her head. In this temporary attire she would put on her make-up before dressing to go out. Glass from a car accident several years earlier had left her with a scar down the left side of her face, and small shards in her forehead had never been removed. For this reason she never left the house without putting on make-up first.

As Sam wrapped the towel around her head the phone rang. It was 6.30 pm. Her sister in Adelaide was home from work and calling to see how she was. They chatted for ten minutes until Sam cut the conversation short—a shadow had fallen across the light from the window and she sensed that she had an uninvited guest. A chill crept over her. But then she remembered the phone. If she was in trouble she could press the button that automatically dialled through to the police and say a two-digit code number to alert them. Harassment, stalking and threats had become a part of Sam's life since Reas had moved out three months ago. Shredded underwear and a slashed doona bore testament to the fact that someone who didn't have her best interests at heart had access to her home. She suspected Reas was behind these incidents but had no proof.

Hesitantly, Sam walked out of the bedroom and into the lounge room to investigate. There was someone at the front door. She spoke to him briefly through the screen door, then grudgingly walked back to the table in the room and rummaged through her small black handbag. Uninvited, he opened the door and followed her into the house.

An exchange of angry words and name calling followed. He pushed and shoved her around the room to emphasise each disparaging word. She screamed at him to stop it, and for a moment he stood back and drew breath. Sam fumbled for a cigarette, lit it, and sat down at the table to steady her shaking legs. He wouldn't join her. She remembered the phone, but he was standing between her and the kitchen. Glancing towards the bedroom door and the other phone on her bedside table, she rose and moved towards the door. The 'man with strong arms and hands' stood menacingly in her path.

As she tried to push past him a fist came down on the side of her head. She stumbled and grabbed for a chair to steady herself. Dazed, she turned to face her attacker and met with blows to her chest and head. He picked her up from the floor and shook her, then threw her against the wall. Bleeding from a wound on her head Sam ducked the next oncoming blow and pushed her assailant aside, momentarily throwing him off balance. She stumbled towards her bedroom. If only she could get to the door, close it and jam it shut, she could phone the police.

The bottom of the bedroom door was sunk into the carpet pile. The door was stuck. Sam couldn't hold him off. Her attacker pushed her into the bedroom and continued his frenzied assault. With blood now in her unfocussed eyes she fell to the floor, helpless against the unremitting blows from her assailant's fists and shoes. As she rolled onto her stomach to protect her now battered body, the blows stopped. She gasped for air in the silent seconds that followed, but her breath was abruptly cut short. Large hands encircled her neck from behind and crushed her airway. When she was still, he released his grip from her throat and dragged her across the passageway into the bathroom. For good measure he wrapped the cord of a hair dryer around her neck three times, and putting his foot on her back for purchase, tightened the cord. He needn't have bothered. Samantha Hall was already dead.

At 6.45 that Friday evening Samantha Hall's father was struck with excruciating indigestion, a complaint he had not suffered from before. He stumbled around the house doubled over in pain, searching for a position that would relieve it. The pain persisted for approximately 20 minutes, then disappeared as quickly as it had come.

The Crime Scene

Early on the morning of Saturday 31 August 1996 a tourist couple came across the body of a woman hidden in bushland several metres from the edge of a car park in Noosa Woods. Not visible from the car park, the body lay off to the side of an ill-defined track through bush densely covered by juvenile wattle (*Acacia*) plants. The flowers of these plants formed a dense gold and green wall along one side of the car park. It is a beautiful and peaceful place to visit and walk through in spring, but on this day it would shortly become a hive of police activity.

Noosa is an upmarket, chic holiday-resort town about two hours' drive north of Queensland's capital, Brisbane. It lies at the top of the Sunshine Coast, a strip of coastal towns popular as holiday and weekend destinations for Brisbane families. This strip of coastline offers a more relaxed beachside experience than the high rise Gold Coast to the south of Brisbane that caters more for international tourist groups and young people seeking sun, sand, surf and sin. Noosa is the jewel of the Sunshine Coast. Its subtropical climate is tempered by the ocean, and it is never truly hot nor very cold. Noosa boasts beautiful beaches, a river, canal developments, nearby everglades and a national park. Despite its renown for being the holiday choice of wealthy international travellers and 'southerners' from Melbourne and Sydney, there are parts of Noosa that cater for the less wealthy. Noosa Heads and its beach accommodate the wealthy, whereas the conjoined Noosaville on the river is more for the everyday person.

The first European to discover the joys of Noosa as a place to 'get away from it all' was convict David Braceful, who regularly escaped custody and headed north to Noosa to live with local Aborigines. Noosa was also a weekend getaway for my family and a large group of friends several times a year in the early 1990s. We rented six to eight townhouses surrounding a pool and sat sipping champagne while our children swam in the pool, played tennis or played with their Super Nintendos. At night children gathered in one townhouse to watch videos and play games—so they said—while the adults played charades and other silly games in another townhouse. Inevitably, someone fell asleep on the floor, snoring with mouth open and drool seeping from its corners, to become the butt of the following day's jokes and a legend to recall on the next trip. We didn't have to drive home, the children were safe, and we could let our hair down or retreat to the peace of our own unit for time out. It was the ultimate break from the prison of everyday reality.

The hub of Noosa is Hastings Street. This tree-lined promenade has a cosmopolitan atmosphere, with streetside cafés, boutiques and expensive accommodation. Only metres behind the seaward side of Hastings Street is Main Beach, one of the few north-facing beaches on the east coast of Australia. To the west, Hastings Street winds into the parkland of Noosa Woods and 'Noosa Spit'.

Officially, Noosa Woods is the first 200–300 metres of this parkland, and its outer margin was once the eastern coastline at the mouth of the Noosa River. Noosa Spit is a man-made sand extension of Noosa Woods. It juts out across the river mouth and forks south-east to protect a canal development, Noosa Sound, built on an island in the mid 1970s. A severe storm shortly after the development was completed caused wave damage to the properties. The sand spit was built in 1978 to protect this island housing development. Tourist maps call the whole area Noosa Woods, but it is commonly called Noosa Spit, or just The Spit. Surrounded by ocean to the north and river to the west and south, this parkland has walking tracks through bushland, public barbecues, and those environmentally friendly but smelly toilets.

The Beach Protection Authority was initially responsible for vegetating the newly constructed Noosa Spit, and planted numerous Horsetail She-oaks (*Casuarina equisetifolia*), Coastal Banksias (*Banksia integrifolia*) and Coastal Wattles (*Acacia longifolia* subsp. *sophorae*). Planting plans were later drawn up for Noosa Woods, then a degraded remnant littoral rainforest, and for the verges of new roads and car parks on Noosa Spit. A local group, Noosa Parks Association Inc., and its sub-group, Greening Noosa, put these plans into action. Several hundred volunteers carried out the first planting stage over two weekends. They planted more Coastal Wattles (Plate 4), plants renowned for being excellent sand-stabilising agents. Subsequent plantings have not included many wattles, but instead have used plants that originally grew in Noosa Woods.

More than ten different species of wattles occur naturally in the Noosa area, but the Coastal Wattle is not one of them. This species naturally occurs on the coasts of Tasmania and along the southern and eastern coasts of continental Australia from Eyre Peninsula in South Australia to southern Queensland. Its northernmost natural occurrence is on sand dunes some 30–40 kilometres south of Noosa.

In August, the wattle bushes bathe much of Noosa Woods in a sea of yellow flowers that play host to a myriad of insects and birds collecting pollen and nectar. The heavily blooming branches drape over the railings surrounding the car parks and, in the bushland behind them, their offspring compete with each other and the weeds for space. Until recently, a small white cross with a plaque stood in a small clearing in this bushland environment where Coastal Wattle once dominated the vegetation. The plaque bore the first name of the woman whose body was found there in 1996, and a message from her children and parents: 'We will never forget you'.

The first official to attend the crime scene on that morning of 31 August was Acting Detective Senior Sergeant (DSS) Brian Cannon, the acting officer in charge of the Noosa Heads Crime Investigation Branch (CIB) at that time. His task was to secure the crime scene and protect it until Scenes-of-Crime officers from Brisbane arrived. He would later oversee the identification of the deceased and the general running of the investigation. Other officers from the Noosa CIB arrived shortly afterwards.

One would assume that the first police officer at a murder scene would have a close look at the body. But this is not the case. There are strict protocols, with specific tasks designated to those specialised in particular areas. The crime scene and surrounding area is first secured by plastic tape, flag markers, paint on the ground or strategic placing of vehicles or guards to prevent evidence being destroyed or contaminated. Officers who secure a crime scene remain at a distance from the actual site, guarding it until Scenes-of-Crime personnel arrive. In Australia, the people who examine the actual crime scene are often specially trained police officers, but in many parts of the world civilian Scenes-of-Crime teams are employed. Their first task is to photograph, measure and survey the scene to produce a scaled map. Then they begin the methodical search for forensic evidence.

In a murder case, the body is not removed until all information regarding its position and its relationship to the environment and associated evidence is recorded. Some specialist forensic scientists may be called to a crime scene while the body is still in place; others will attend a crime scene after a body has been removed. What order they attend a scene is determined by the type of case and the crime scene protocol in a particular jurisdiction. For example, if a body has begun to decompose, a forensic entomologist should be called in while the body is still in place. They will collect insects (mostly flies and beetles), their larvae (e.g. fly maggots) and pupae from the body, under the body and the surrounding area. From the types of insects present, the knowledge of their life cycles, the context of the situation and the weather variables (mainly temperature) while the body was decomposing, an entomologist can determine the time of death.

In an ideal situation, a forensic botanist and palynologist should be the first specialist forensic scientists to attend an outdoor crime scene. This is so that plant and pollen evidence is not destroyed or contaminated by other investigators trampling over the area. However, in the majority of jurisdictions palynology is not used because investigators don't know about it. If they do, it is often an afterthought, or officers at the crime scene collect the samples for the palynologist. Hopefully this will change as the use of forensic palynology and botany becomes more common.

In the UK this is already changing. Patricia Wiltshire, who has worked as a forensic botanist and palynologist in the UK and Europe for more than 10 years, is called to crime scenes early in an investigation. In the Soham case, Ian Huntley, the school caretaker who killed two young girls in 2002, was brought to justice primarily by evidence collected and analysed by Patricia. Although a photographer and several other crime scene personnel had already approached the scene before Patricia arrived, they didn't go anywhere near the bodies until after she had completed her work. Fortunately they didn't take the same path to the crime scene as Huntley did. If they had, much of the botanical and palynological evidence eventually collected by Patricia would have been missed or contaminated.

Although some of the forensic officers from Scientific Section in Brisbane who attended the Noosa crime scene knew of palynology, it wasn't routine practice to call in a palynologist or collect palynology samples.

Television news reports of crime scenes under examination often show people in identical disposable overalls, booties, gloves and face masks. This protective attire prevents fibre and DNA contamination and the transfer of other particles from investigators' shoes and clothing. There's no point in turning up to a crime scene in high heels and a tight skirt hoping to impress a cute policeman.

'We've only got extra large left mate', seems to be my lot when I'm given a disposable overall. With the crutch hanging between my knees, sample collection is a challenge, and attractive I am not.

External to the crime scene examination are the investigation personnel, who deal with people and objects related to a case. The official names of the groups that deal with different parts of a case vary in different States and countries. For murder cases in Queensland, the local CIB officers, the Homicide Investigation Squad and forensic officers from Scientific Section are all involved. In this particular case the officer who first handled the general administrative side of the investigation, DSS Brian Cannon, and the officers designated to be the Arrest Team and Exhibits Officer, were from the Noosa CIB. The Exhibits Officer collated and kept records of items collected from the crime scene, or from any other thing or person suspected to be related to the crime. This person also kept a record of where exhibits were sent for forensic analysis. The Arrest Team dealt directly with the people side of the investigation—the interviewing of relatives, friends, other witnesses and any person suspected of being involved in the crime. The latter is often reported as a person 'assisting police with their investigation'.

At the murder scene in Noosa Woods there was no evidence that a struggle had taken place, but marks in the sand suggested that the body had been dragged to its deposition site. No personal belongings were found at the crime scene to identify the deceased.

Police and the media have a love–hate relationship, but in truth neither functions well without the other. At 2 pm on Saturday 31 August 1996, news programs reported the discovery of an unknown woman's body in Noosa Woods. They carried a description of the woman and distinguishing features that police thought might cause someone to come forward and help to identify her. Of prime importance were the two names, Michael and Corey, tattooed on her right arm. The response was good. Noosa CIB received phone calls from concerned friends of Samantha Hall. Samantha had not joined them at the Mt Pleasant Hotel the night before as she had promised, and Michael and Corey, the names of her children, were tattooed on her right arm. Police moved their investigation to Gympie.

Every Parent's Nightmare

Gympie is a major provincial city about an hour's drive inland from Noosa and two hours' drive north of Brisbane. It is famous for being the centre of Queensland's first gold rush, in 1867. Today it's the centre of the Mary River Valley agricultural district and services about 60 000 people, of which approximately one-quarter live in the town itself. Samantha Hall's parents, Lyn and Malcolm, live on a small farm outside Gympie.

Lyn and Malcolm didn't hear the 2 pm news report that Saturday, but two hours later they learnt from a friend in Brisbane that the body of a woman found in Noosa earlier that day fitted the description of their younger daughter, Samantha. The heartbreak and gut-wrenching agony they felt was tinged with the faint hope that their friend was mistaken. Sam would never go to Noosa with a stranger; she wouldn't even unlock the door of her house to a stranger.

The distraught parents spent the next two hours in total disbelief. They made phone calls to friends who they hoped might know where Sam was. In their hearts they wanted to believe she was still alive, but rationally they knew that the body tattooed with their grandsons' names was that of their daughter. Reality finally struck Lyn and Malcolm early that evening when the police phoned to say they were coming out to their farm to speak to them.

Get the boys...get the boys...was resounding in Lyn's mind. Why, on this weekend, did Reas have them? They must get the boys from their paternal grandparents before Sam's death was confirmed and made public. After a difficult phone conversation with Reas' parents, they agreed to let Malcolm collect the boys. Within minutes he was on his way to their house.

When Malcolm arrived at Reas' parents' place, Sam's small boys, aged four and six, were watching television. They were watching the news report that a woman, with the names Michael and Corey tattooed on her arm, had been found dead in Noosa. Alarmed at this, Malcolm gathered them up as calmly as he could, hoping they had not been paying attention to the report. But the elder boy had. As they walked to the car he asked Malcolm where his mummy was and if it was her that had been found dead. Malcolm said he didn't know, but that they would soon find out where she was. As he helped the boys into the car and wrapped blankets around them to keep them warm on the drive back to the farm, the dread in the pit of his stomach weighed heavily on him. This little boy, his lovely Sam's son, knew deep down that his mummy was not coming home.

Malcolm and the boys arrived back at the farm only minutes after the police had arrived. The boys went into the bedroom that Lyn and Malcolm had set up especially for their weekend visits. They played while their grandparents spoke to the police in the kitchen. The conversation that ensued dashed any hope Lyn and Malcolm had that Sam was still alive. Her car, a Toyota Corolla, had been found abandoned in the car park of a Gympie nightclub and the police description of the body left them in little doubt that it was their Sam. The police would take them to Brisbane that night to identify the body.

While waiting for another police car to arrive to take them to the Brisbane morgue, Lyn and Malcolm put their grandsons to bed and arranged for friends who lived nearby to come over and stay with them. They left for Brisbane shortly after 9 pm that Saturday evening.

Early the next morning Lyn and Malcolm Hall identified the body of their 27-year-old daughter Samantha Jane. It was 12.03 am on 1 September 1996, and that year, it was Fathers' Day. Their beautiful young daughter's body was black and blue from the waist up. The white gold chain with the Blue John pendant they had given her for her twenty-first birthday, her watch and a tiny nose stud were not on her body. She wore these items of jewellery all the time—had they been stolen from her body or might they be found where she had been murdered? Samantha's head had been badly bashed, there were three deep furrows encircling her neck, and both her thumbs and one finger had been broken. The battered hands were in plastic bags—her grieving parents couldn't even hold her hand.

It was not only the injuries Samantha sustained in her battle for life that shocked her parents. Lyn immediately saw evidence that confirmed what she had suspected all along. Sam didn't go to Noosa voluntarily. There was no make-up on the face of her battered body. Her ritual of shower, make-up and then dressing had been interrupted. Lyn and Malcolm were convinced that Sam had been murdered in her own home—after coming out of the shower and before she had time to put on her make-up. At that time she would be wrapped in two towels—one around her head and another sarong-style around her body. Sam's body was dressed in her new jeans, new black boots, and an old T-shirt that she wouldn't voluntarily wear outside the house. No blood was on her clothing or body. Was she dressed by her murderer after she died?—and did this person shower her before dressing her?

Five minutes into their journey back home from Brisbane with the police, Lyn and Malcolm told officers accompanying them of their 'evidence', and that as far as they were concerned there was only one suspect—Reas. They were sure, although they had no positive proof, that he was the person responsible for the harassment Sam had suffered the past few months. They knew of his violence, but most chilling of all was their memory of his threat to Sam that he would kill her one day.

In her inimitably candid way Lyn insisted that the police arrest Reas as soon as possible. But police don't operate that way. They rarely arrest a suspect on circumstantial evidence. If the evidence is slim, a clever lawyer will get a suspect off a charge—guilty or not. Sadly, truth does not always prevail in our justice system. The more evidence the police can gather, the more likely a guilty person is to be convicted. This explained, Lyn and Malcolm resigned themselves to waiting for enough evidence to be collected before Sam's killer could be arrested—be it Reas or some unknown person.

One of my students, a high-ranking police officer, once referred to pollen evidence as another brick in the wall. He meant that many types of forensic science may be used to build a case. Each line of evidence provides part of a puzzle or a wall that, when complete, will surround and fence in the person who committed the crime. Missing bricks are but gifts to the defence counsel.

The investigating officers didn't discount the possibility that Reas was Sam's killer. Even if he had been a model partner, his possible involvement in Sam's death would not have been overlooked. Police are aware of the statistics. A recent conference for domestic violence and injury-prevention workers reported that 'about 125 women and girls were murdered each year in Australia. All but 14 were killed by someone they knew, and about 70% were the result of domestic violence' (*The West Australian*, 26 November 2003). The article, entitled 'Men murder their property', further reported that there were patterns among the subgroup of men who killed their partners. They treat their partners as property, and have a history of domestic violence and threatening to kill. I have often wondered whether, if these figures were common knowledge, men who killed their partners would think twice before doing so.

Until I became involved in forensic science, it never occurred to me that the majority of women homicide victims were killed by their partners or former partners. The penny only dropped when I was called to a murder scene in Perth, Western Australia, a couple of years later, in 1999. A woman had been bashed to death in the driveway of the family home in the early hours of the morning. I had been asked to attend the scene to collect soil and plant samples from the garden near where the body had been found. The police hoped that if they found a suspect, I could compare pollen from the garden samples with pollen on the suspect's clothing or shoes.

I'd arrived several hours after the body had been removed but the pool of blood on the cement driveway was still there. The police had briefed me on the scene as it was when they arrived and on what the husband had told them. As I recall, the husband had found the deceased lying on the driveway, dressed only in her nightgown, as he had been leaving for the airport early that morning. He had slept in another room that night so as not to disturb her when he left. He suspected that his wife had been awoken by a noise outside and, thinking it was him leaving for the airport, had gone outside to farewell him. Instead, she had met with an intruder who battered her to death. To all intents and purposes this was a normal happy family and the husband was suitably distraught. After the briefing we had discussed where an intruder might have entered and left the property and what soil and pollen samples should be collected.

As I noted down the proposed sample locations, the officer said quietly, 'But of course, we can't discount hubby'. I was stunned—this was a neat suburban house in a quiet street and the couple had a small child. It didn't fit my television-inspired image of domestic homicide. But television crime series and reality have little in common.

My pollen evidence was never used. During the following week the deceased's husband made several attempts to commit suicide. He had murdered his wife.

Such scenarios are commonplace to police who investigate homicides. The partner or estranged partner of a deceased woman is high on their suspect list. Samantha Hall's case was no different. Police considered Reas a 'person of interest' and were keen to meet with him but, as often happens, they had no need to look for the former partner of the deceased. While Lyn and Malcolm were living through their nightmare late that Saturday afternoon, a distressed Reas walked into the Gympie police station. He had heard the news. It was shortly after 6.00 pm and Detective Sergeant Paul Zohn, the chief investigating officer, had just begun to interview one of Samantha Hall's friends.

Reas produced photographs of Sam from his wallet. Paul was unable to confirm that the woman in the photos was the woman whose body had been found at Noosa earlier in the day—he hadn't seen the body close-up, and it was yet to be officially identified.

Paul decided to conduct a formal taped interview. In it, Reas asserted that he hadn't seen Sam since 6.00 pm Friday, the previous evening. He alleged that she had collected him from the Woolworths car park after his car had broken down. He didn't know where she had gone after that. She wasn't with him. He'd spent the evening in Gympie. To corroborate his whereabouts that Friday evening Reas detailed the path he had walked to buy cigarettes. The receipt, with the time of purchase printed on it, was in his wallet.

During the interview, Reas claimed that he'd been concerned about Sam's whereabouts since early that Saturday morning. He had wanted to collect more clothes for the boys, but when he'd phoned Sam she hadn't answered her phone. Then he'd phoned her parents. They didn't know where she was. Eventually he had asked one of Sam's close girlfriends to accompany him to the house. What he didn't tell police was that when they went to the house that Saturday morning, Sam's girlfriend had noticed blood on a light switch. When she brought this to his attention he had wiped it off.

Reas also provided police with information about Sam's recent relationship, painting an unflattering picture. He told them that she had been in a steady relationship for almost two months but inferred that she was also seeing other men at the same time. Because her car was found parked outside a Gympie nightclub, he intimated that she may have met someone in the nightclub and gone with them to another club in Noosa. Police had already considered that scenario. They now had another 'person of interest'—Matt, Sam's boyfriend. They would interview him as soon as possible.

The receipt from his purchase of cigarettes and his broken-down car provided Reas with a tenuous alibi. Helpfully, he agreed to supply a saliva sample for DNA analysis, fully aware that it would be compared with DNA analyses of trace evidence found during the course of the investigation—for example, traces of skin under the victim's fingernails and body fluids or blood. Reas had wounds on one hand that he asserted were sustained at work. Subsequent enquiries revealed that he did injure his hand at work that Saturday morning.

The interview Paul Zohn conducted with Reas that Saturday night took almost six hours. During that time the police drove the victim's parents to Brisbane to positively identify the body, and the Scenes-of-Crime specialists from Scientific Section were methodically examining the neat and tidy home in Gympie that Samantha Hall had lived in with her two sons.

Although the police had no reason at that time to connect Samantha's home with her murder, technically, it was another crime scene. The term 'crime scene' applies not only to places where a criminal incident took place, but also to any other places that may reveal evidence that points to, or rules out, suspects or events. In this case, the place where the body was found and where the victim and suspects lived were all crime scenes.

More Crime Scenes

Crime-scene examiners work on the premise of Locard's Exchange Principle. Dr Edmond Locard established the world's first crime laboratory, the Technical Police Laboratory in Lyons, France, in 1910. He was also the first person to mention pollen as a likely source of physical evidence. Locard believed that whenever two objects (or people) come into contact, there is a cross-transfer of material. Examination of this material could reveal an association between a suspect and a location or a victim.

After studying the dust on clothing and how it is transferred to other articles, Locard reported that 'The microscopic dusts which cover our clothes and our bodies are silent yet certain and reliable witnesses of each of our actions and contacts'.[1] In other words, a person who commits a crime will leave something at the scene or take something away from the scene. The 'something' may be relatively obvious, such as personal belongings or impressions of shoes or tools, or it may be trace evidence that can only be seen with a microscope or by using special forensic techniques and tools. For example, a variety of powders can be dusted onto surfaces to highlight fingerprints, and special chemicals are used to detect the presence of blood.

Luminol, a blood-enhancing chemical, can detect minute amounts of blood and is especially useful when a crime scene has been 'cleaned up'. When sprayed onto blood, Luminol reacts with the iron in haemoglobin, the oxygen-carrying protein in red blood cells, to form another substance. The energy from this reaction is released as a blue-green luminescence that can only be seen in the dark —not in light, as portrayed in some television series! The intensity of the glow decreases after about 30 seconds. Special cameras capture images of the luminescence and record its position. Luminol may also react with some paints, cleaning products, metals and some plants, but the reaction differs in intensity from that produced by its contact with traces of blood. Chemiluminescent chemicals like Luminol can detect blood traces that are many years old, but they can't determine the age of blood. This means that traces of blood found at a crime scene may not necessarily be related to the crime. They may be from innocent cuts or blood noses many years beforehand.

As they had done at the Noosa crime scene, the police examiners methodically photographed the inside of the house and searched for evidence. Along otherwise spotless floor tiles of the living room and hallway there were double black streaks, like those left by dragging black shoes or boots, that led to the internal garage door. A tiny nose stud was found lodged in the grid of a drain in the bathroom floor. The police collected hairs and fibres from the bedding and tested articles of clothing and floors for the presence of blood. They found what appeared to be blood stains on the bedroom and loungeroom floors, and traces of blood on a T-shirt in the washing machine, a tea-towel in the kitchen, a hairdryer and the lip of a wastepaper basket in the bathroom, and the floor in the garage. The fibres, hairs, blood swabs and other evidence collected would be sent to the relevant forensic scientists for analysis. Blood samples would be collected from Samantha's children, her boyfriend Matt, and her former de facto partner Reas Holden for DNA analysis and comparison.

By Sunday morning the police had two lines of evidence indicating that Samantha Hall had not been murdered in Noosa where her body was found: these were the blood in her home and her parents' observations when they identified her body. The pathologist who conducted the post-mortem on Samantha's body provided further evidence to support this theory. This was the position of hypostasis in her body.

Homeostasis is the stable state in which an organism maintains its internal environment. In humans this includes a constant level and pressure of body fluids, including blood. When a person dies, blood settles under the influence of gravity and causes discolouration of the skin in body parts closest to the ground. This differential distribution of blood is termed hypostasis, and the apparent bruising it causes is described as lividity. If a person dies lying on their back, hypostasis will occur on the back of their body; if they die hanging, blood will concentrate in the lower parts of their limbs. After a period of time the hypostasis becomes fixed, and if it is fixed in a different aspect to the position the body was found in, it indicates that the body has been moved after death.

The pattern of settled blood (hypostasis) in Samantha Hall's body was not consistent with the position in which her body had been found. From this the pathologist was able to determine that she had been dead for quite some time when her body was placed in the bushland of Noosa Woods. The deep grooves around Samantha's neck and related physical evidence suggested that the cause of death was strangulation.

By Sunday afternoon the investigators had a cause of death and strong evidence that the murder had taken place in the victim's home. But there were still many unanswered questions. What did the murderer bash and strangle the victim with? The deep grooves around her neck may have been made by a belt, or possibly by the cord of a hairdryer in the bathroom, but a heavy implement was used on other parts of her body. The pathologist found depressions in the victim's skull consistent with a blunt instrument—but no likely weapon had been found. How was the body transported to Noosa? And why was Samantha Hall's car parked at the local nightclub?

At this stage in the investigation, with no murder weapon and two possible suspects, there were several cars of interest—Samantha's Corolla, the station wagon Reas drove and the car belonging to Sam's boyfriend Matt. Reas' car was still in the Woolworths car park, its battery terminals and cables damaged—possibly by a hard object. Officers from Scientific Section examined it, and similarly examined Matt's car at his workplace, looking for any items or other evidence that might help in the investigation. Nothing of interest was found in either vehicle. Samantha Hall's Corolla was taken to Police Headquarters in Brisbane to be examined in detail by forensic officers from Scientific Section.

Senior Sergeant Brad Hall examined the Corolla. He used sheets of adhesive paper to take 'tape-lifts' from inside the car to collect surface fibres, dirt and dust, then vacuumed each section of the car separately. To prevent airborne contamination he used a special vacuum cleaner with an attachment that pre-filters the air. A filter-paper extraction system allows the material vacuumed from each area to be removed from the vacuum cleaner and placed in a separate bag. The machine is then reloaded and another area is vacuumed. This separation of potential evidence is vital because evidence found in the passenger side of a car may have different implications if it were to be found in the driver's side of a car.

Of intense interest to Brad Hall were two wattle flowers—one found in the front driver's side of the car and one found on the rear of the car near the numberplate. Wattles were flowering profusely where the body had been found. Could the Corolla, Samantha Hall's own car, have been used to drive her body from Gympie to Noosa Woods?

There are estimated to be up to nearly 1000 species of wattle (*Acacia*) in Australia. These hardy plants are widespread across the continent and can be found in almost all types of habitats. Like most places in Australia, several species of wattle grew in Gympie.

Police speculated that if wattle species growing at the crime scene were different to those in Gympie, it might be possible to identify what wattle species produced the flowers found in Samantha's car and therefore what town the flowers came from. A botanist could identify what wattle species grew in Gympie and Noosa, but identifying the flowers would not be so simple. How could this be done? Dried wattle flowers from different species often look very similar. Perhaps their pollen could be used. But only if pollen from the wattle species at Noosa and Gympie could be distinguished from each other.

The study of the structural features of pollen, known as pollen morphology, is a science in itself. Like other sciences, it has special terminology that is used worldwide. This ensures that all palynologists describe and identify pollen the same way—well that's the theory. The ability to recognise small physical differences in pollen from closely related species is essential in forensic pollen analysis. However, this ability is only one of the many skills forensic palynologists need. They must also be able to interpret pollen samples. For example, they need to be able to answer questions like: What does the presence and relative frequency of a particular pollen type in a sample mean? Was it carried to the place it finally settled by wind or some other means? Is its parent plant common in the area, or is it rare or absent? In short, to answer these kinds of crucial crime-busting questions, a successful pollen analyst must know all about the birds and the bees—the sex life of plants.

The Birds and the Bees

Food, then attracting the opposite sex—or maybe it's the other way around—seem to be the male animal's prime goals in life. Whichever way it is, males put a lot of energy into developing special skills or adornments to compete with other males for the favours of females of their species. Male birds display their glorious colours, their dancing expertise or their ability to build a spectacular nest. Male mammals use their size, strength and physical attractiveness to ensure that their genetic material is perpetuated. But it isn't just animals that try to impress the opposite sex. In the plant world sex is just as competitive. Many flowers, for example, are a plant's way of advertising for go-betweens (insects and animals) to assist with their sex life.

When lecturing to students, police and community groups, I'm uncomfortable when we get to the section about the sex life of plants. It's not the sex bit that worries me, but the squirms and shuffling of feet. They know what is coming. A boring botany lesson like those they endured in their early years of schooling about the structure of flowers. I slept through all of mine—science was after lunch. This lack of attention proved unbearably embarrassing many years later.

It was the early 1980s and I had completed my three-year geology course at the University of Western Australia. My Honours project on the palynology of 40 million-year-old lignites (low-grade coal) was almost finished. It had crossed my mind that if my project was about pollen, albeit fossil pollen, then I should refresh my memory about the biological role of pollen—but I was pregnant with my first child and many things I should have done didn't get done. Then came Halloween and an invitation to a party run by those lofty beings, the doctoral students. At that time there were no worries about drink driving, and the aroma of illegal substances was thick in the air. I, however, was sober, straight and heavy with child. My husband had left my side briefly to find me a soft drink, and I stood alone in the milling crowd on the back lawn. Robyn, the student running the party, was from the USA and I admired her immensely. She was vibrant, interesting and always made one feel important. Seeing me standing alone she embarked on some small talk about my project. She gleaned from my answers to her questions that only a tiny amount of lignite could yield thousands of pollen grains, and that most dark to light grey sedimentary rocks also contained a lot of pollen.

'That's amazing', Robyn said with her usual enthusiasm, 'but how do so many pollen grains get into the rocks?' she asked. I gulped. I wasn't sure, except that it had something to do with the basic research I should have done. Damn, why didn't I listen in class?

'Well, I think it's that plants produce a lot of them', I replied after a pause that I hoped would seem learned. My stomach suddenly felt queasy.

'But why do they produce so much?' she persisted. The queasiness was rolling itself into knots in my stomach.

'Well, it's got something to do with…er…um…er…sorry about this, but I feel a bit faint', I confessed. Robyn was concerned. With a helping hand I made it into the house and onto a chair. After the obligatory wet face cloth, resting my chin on my chest—the soon-to-be 10 lb baby was obstructing the recommended head between the legs trick—and a cup of tea, all was well and any talk of pollen had long been forgotten.

In retrospect I'm not sure whether my stomach knots and faintness were due to maternity stress or because I was in a difficult situation and about to be proven ignorant. My uneasiness at answering Robyn's questions must've been obvious. Did she think I was trying to get out of answering the question? I've lost contact with her, but if ever we meet again we'll have a good laugh and I'll invite her to one of my presentations on forensic palynology where the reasons why plants produce so much pollen are discussed in full.

My first talk on palynology to non-palynologists was an introductory seminar in the then Geography Department at the University of Western Australia. This was my debut, my chance to prove that I was worthy of the prestigious Postdoctoral Research Fellowship I had won from a large field of applicants. The title of my talk was the same as the title of my postdoctoral application: 'Old Guys, Young Guys and Bad Guys'. The senior academic of some 30 years experience who was preparing the flyer to advertise the talk was puzzled.

'So what does the title mean?' he queried.

'I work with fossil pollen, modern pollen and pollen that helps to solve crimes', I replied. It made sense to me. But no, he still didn't get it.

'Why guys?' he queried.

'All pollen are boys', I stated.

'They can't *all* be boys', he replied in disbelief.

'Well they are', I informed him. A brief lesson on the sex life of plants followed. I was initially stunned at his lack of knowledge, but my own ignorance and embarrassment years ago came flooding back as we spoke. I went home and rewrote my seminar presentation.

Today, the biological role of pollen and its methods of dispersal are integral parts of my presentations, even to audiences with academic backgrounds in the biological sciences. If I don't do this, some puzzled person asks that scary question at the end of my talk: 'Why do plants produce so much pollen?' I like to save them the embarrassment.

All plants produce either pollen or spores as part of their reproductive cycle. Pollen, the fine yellow dust produced by flowers, is best known for the runny noses, sneezes and wheezes it can cause during spring. These misery-producing microscopic particles are the sperm of the plant world. Pollen carries the male sex cells of seed plants—the flowering plants and plants that produce cones, such as conifers (e.g. pines). The more primitive plants—the ferns and mosses—produce spores. Although spores are similar in size and distribution to pollen, they are asexual and have a different reproductive function to pollen. To sexually reproduce, ferns and mosses require two generations. When the spores fall to the ground they germinate and develop into a small second generation plant that produces both male and female cells. When released, the male cells swim to the female cells to effect fertilisation. This is why ferns and mosses prefer moist conditions.

Most flowering plants have both male and female organs contained in the same flower (see diagram on page 40). But some of the more ancient flowering plants, like the she-oaks (e.g. *Casuarina*), bear separate male and female flowers on the same tree, or a tree may only bear male or female flowers (i.e. the tree will be either male or female). Similarly, the cone-bearing conifers either produce both male and female cones on the one plant or each plant bears either male or female cones.

The female reproductive organ, the pistil, consists of an ovary containing one or more ovules—the female sex cells or eggs—and a stigma and style. The stigma, the sticky receptive organ that pollen is caught on, is connected to the ovary by the style. Before fertilisation, the nucleus in the ovule divides to produce a number of different cells. One cell will become the actual egg cell

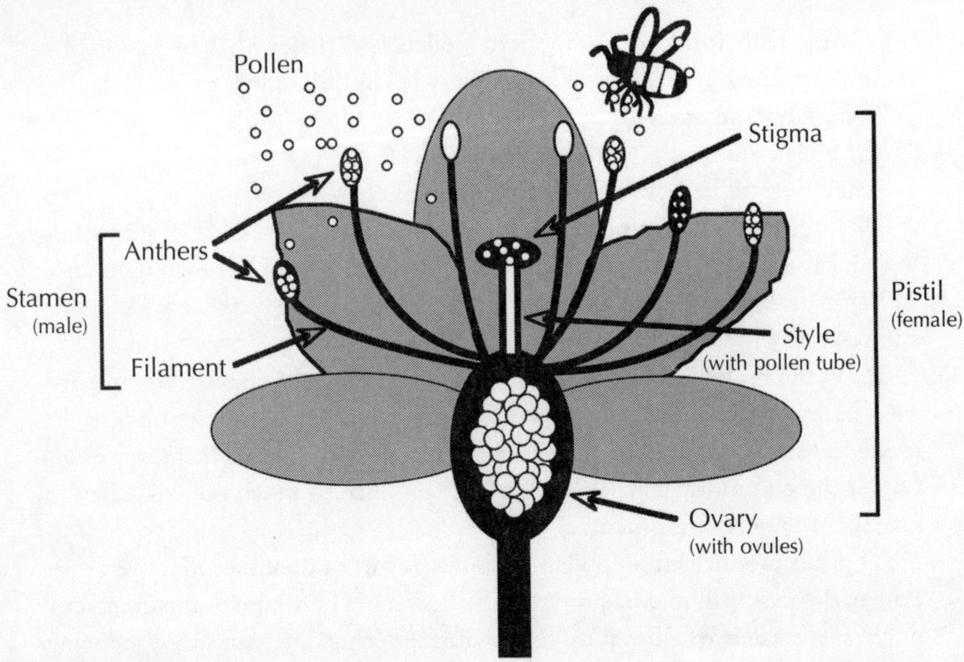

Cross-section of a hypothetical flower *showing the male and female organs.*

and the remaining cells will eventually become part of the food store of the seed after fertilisation.

The stamens, the male parts of a flower, each consist of a stalk, called the filament, with a small sac, the anther, at its tip. Pollen grains are produced inside the anthers, and each grain contains two male nuclei. Pollen grains are, of course, tiny and invisible to the human eye. Nevertheless, they vary enormously in size and shape and they have exceptionally varied and beautiful adornments. These elaborate displays of maleness are not for attracting females, as in the animal world, but are to assist them to travel in search of a mate.

When a pollen grain lands on the stigma of a flower of the same species, one of its two nuclei (the tube nucleus) grows a pollen tube from an opening in the pollen grain. The pollen tube grows down through the tissue of the style to the ovary and enters an ovule through a tiny hole in the ovule cell wall (micropyle). The other nucleus (generative nucleus) divides to form two male nuclei, and both travel down the pollen tube to the ovule. Fertilisation takes place when one of the male nuclei fuses with the female egg cell in the ovule. The other male nucleus fuses with the central nucleus of the remaining female cells in the ovule to form the endosperm, the food store in the ovule (now called a seed) that will provide the developing plant with nutrition until it is large enough to produce its own food. With a little lateral thinking, the route the male plant cell takes is not so different from that of an animal male sex cell.

The sex life of plants is reminiscent of the Victorian era. The females stay at home and wait for a knock on the door. They reject all offers of unsavoury suitors and only open the door to boys of their own kind. The boys, on the other hand, are handicapped, because they have no way of transporting themselves at will to vie for the hand of a lady. Instead they must catch a ride with the wind or on insects or small animals and take the chance that they'll reach the right door.

So what happens to pollen if it ends up on the wrong sort of flower? Say a daisy pollen grain finds its way to the stigma of a rose. It won't be welcome. Pollen grains and stigmas of flowers from the same species have a mutual recognition system, and only pollen of the same species will be able to form a viable pollen tube right down the style to the ovary. Studies show that pollen from other plants may start to form a pollen tube down the style, but the tube will stop forming well before it reaches the ovary. Only some very closely related plants, for example species of the same genus that differ in only a few respects, may interbreed. In such cases, the seed that is produced grows into a hybrid plant that bears a mixture of both parents' characteristics. Cultivars, plants that are purposely cross-pollinated by horticulturalists to produce larger flowers or fruit, resistance to particular diseases or other desirable characters, are hybrids. Many hybrids are sterile. An interesting example was brought to my attention recently. The pollen of a hybrid bore no similarity to the pollen of either parent plant nor any other species of that particular plant family. It was an elliptical blob with no openings for male sex cells to emerge from, and no features to aid its transport. It was pretend pollen.

Catching a ride and not being able to tell the cab driver where you want to go is a very inefficient way of getting around. It would take many random rides, perhaps thousands or even millions in a large city, for the cab driver to randomly stop at the place you wished to go. This is the dilemma plants face. To hedge their bets they produce enormous amounts of pollen, so that at least a few grains will get lucky. Unfortunately, most of the boys don't reach their intended destination; instead they end up as part of soil and dust. They fall onto any surface exposed to the air. It serves them right for playing the field, but it is this aspect of the sex life of plants that makes pollen such an excellent forensic tool. In even a small amount of soil or dust there will be hundreds, perhaps thousands of pollen grains that may have come from many different species, and from numerous individuals of each species. Some may have been carried there on the bodies of flower visitors such as small creatures, others may have been light enough to have travelled on the air currents, and other, heavier pollen, will have dropped to the ground from flowers close by.

The total amount and types of pollen found in any one soil or sediment sample is called a pollen assemblage. Palynology would be quite simple if all the pollen in a pollen assemblage came only from plants that grew at the site the sample was collected from. But this is not the case. Pollen assemblages recovered from a soil sample will also contain pollen from plants that grow in nearby areas and disperse their pollen by wind. This mixture of pollen from different places is one of the most important things forensic palynologists must take into account when interpreting a pollen assemblage from an unknown locality. They must also recognise that if a lot of pollen grains from one plant type occur in the assemblage, this does not necessarily mean that a lot of plants of that type grow at that locality. Confusing? Yes, but not if we know a few basic facts about how pollen is dispersed and its rates of production, and adjust our interpretations accordingly.

The method a plant uses to disperse its pollen to effect pollination—the transfer of male cells to female receptive organs—will determine how much pollen it produces. This will, in turn, establish how useful a particular pollen type will be in a forensic investigation.

The least useful type of pollen for forensic purposes is pollen that is dispersed by water (hydrogamous). Many submerged plants rely on flowing water or currents to transport their pollen. The chances of a pollen grain reaching its intended destination by this method are not good, so each anther produces thousands of pollen grains. However, because pollen of water-pollinating plants needs no attractive features to catch a ride, nor thick walls to stop it from drying out, it is generally very small, with thin unornamented walls, and doesn't preserve well in sediment. If it does, the chemicals used to prepare pollen samples will often destroy it.

The type of pollination that we can actually see happening and that is the most interesting is zoogamy (*zoo* = animal in Greek)—the transport of pollen by insects and small animals. More than half the flowering plants of the world use this method. The anthers and stigma of zoogamous plants commonly mature at different times to guard against self-pollination. Bees, ants, beetles, butterflies, flies and other insects, lizards, birds, bats and other small mammals are unwitting cab drivers as they visit a flower to collect nectar or pollen, then flit onto another flower. As they brush past anthers, pollen sticks to various parts of their bodies and travels with them to the next flower, where it may be brushed onto a mature stigma.

Zoogamous flowers are usually quite conspicuous or decorative and have canny ways of attracting pollinators. Many produce nectar for insects and animals to feed on, and some even have nectar guides, such as dots or lines on the petals, to lead the pollinators to the nectar glands. Some of these markings are only visible to us in ultraviolet light, but are clearly visible to insects in normal sunlight. These special 'roads' leading to the nectar glands are strategically positioned so that animals feeding on nectar will inadvertently collect and transport pollen. Mammal-pollinated flowers are often prostrate (lie along the ground) and have strong-smelling nectar, whereas bird-pollinated flowers are large, bright and strong enough to hold a bird's weight. These plants produce large amounts of nectar during daylight hours to induce the birds to feed upon them.

On a recent trip to Noosa I attempted to take photos of wattle flowers and the pollinators that visit them. There were plenty of pollinators, but they didn't stay long enough for me to focus my telephoto lens and snap. I'd get something in focus and another pollinator, a bee or a wasp, would buzz my head. Dancing about to prevent any contact with the unpleasant end of said insects, the pollinators I was stalking on the flowers bugged off. The number of different insects and birds that visited the same tree was astounding. There was even a worm feeding on pollen. It was the only visitor to the wattle flowers that posed for my photographs (see Plate 12).

Zoogamous pollination is relatively reliable, so each anther produces only 100 to 1000 pollen grains. To put this magnitude into perspective, check out how small the anthers are in a daisy or other common flowering plant, and imagine 1000 pollen grains inside each anther, then multiply that by the number of anthers. The total number of pollen grains one flower may produce is staggering.

Zoogamous pollen usually has highly ornamented thick walls that preserve well. The ornamentation is often designed for easy attachment to insect or animal legs or bodies. The forensic potential of pollen from zoogamous plants is excellent. It's heavy, and if it falls to the ground it won't travel far from its parent plant. The distinctive ornamentation and wall structure means that zoogamous pollen can usually be identified to the species level, and sometimes to the actual plant that produced it. If even a small amount of this pollen type is found on a person's clothing, it indicates that they have either brushed past the plant that produced it, or have come in contact with soil near the plant or with an object that has had contact with the soil or plant.

Pollination by wind is the method used by many of the more ancient plants, such as the cone-bearing conifers, cycads and ginkgos, and she-oaks and many forest trees. More recently evolved plants, such as grasses, sedges and saltbushes, also disperse their pollen with the aid of wind. All ferns, mosses and fungi—the spore-producing plants—use wind to disperse their spores. Plants that use this method of pollination are called anemophilous (*anemos* = wind in Greek).

Wind is the least efficient method of pollination, so wind-pollinated plants compensate by producing vast quantities of light, aerodynamic pollen. Individual anthers may produce between 10 000 and 100 000 grains. Cannabis, for example, produces about 70 000 pollen grains per anther, and a whole plant may produce several hundred million grains. In many European countries and parts of North America and New Zealand, the 'pollen rain' from forests can form a visible cloud. Aside from creating severe problems for asthmatics and allergy sufferers, as it settles it coats cars, windows and anything left outside with a golden layer. As very few wind-transported pollen grains reach their intended destination, they are the most common pollen type found in soil and dust.

How far a pollen grain will travel by wind from its parent plant depends on how long it takes for it to sink to the ground. The sinking rate of a particular pollen type is determined by aerodynamic factors—the shape, size and weight of the grains. Pine pollen has balloon-like bladders to keep it aloft for long periods of time, and some pollen grains are shaped like frisbees—very thin discs that have reduced wind resistance. Studies conducted in the northern hemisphere show that about 95% of wind-transported pollen will sink to the ground between 25 metres and 2 kilometres from its parent plant. The other 5% will sink somewhere between 2 kilometres and hundreds of kilometres away from its source, some even rising high into the atmosphere in thermals and coming back down to Earth as 'seeds' of raindrops. No, this is not aerial fertilisation. Atmospheric water vapour condenses around small dust particles, including pollen, to form water droplets that, when massed together, form clouds and eventually raindrops. Some pollen can remain aloft for days or even weeks. The pollen of rye grass, one of the major causes of hay fever and allergic rhinitis, can remain afloat for weeks.

Most plants seek to transport their pollen to the stigmas of other plants to ensure genetic diversity, but some plants are not averse to keeping it all in the family. These are autogamous plants (*auto* = self in Greek)—that is, they pollinate themselves. To this end the anthers and stigma of a flower mature at the same time. Many self-pollinating flowers have adaptive mechanisms that ensure that their own pollen reaches their own stigma. Others rely on wind and animals to transport their pollen the short distance from their anthers to their stigma. As this is an efficient method of pollination, anthers produce less than 100 pollen grains each. Pollen produced by self-pollinating plants may be found in soil near the plants, but it will be exceptionally rare in comparison with pollen from plants using other types of pollination. Although rare, if this type of pollen is found in a forensic sample it may be a good indicator of a particular site or vegetation type.

An even more efficient method of plant incest is closed pollination. Among botanists, plants that use this method of pollination are referred to as cleistogamous, a word derived from the Greek word meaning 'closed marriage'. Cleistogamous plants pollinate themselves without the flowers ever having to open. This saves the plant energy, as it doesn't have to produce conspicuous flowers. Pollen produced by cleistogamous plants is often relatively large, with little surface ornamentation. Getting lucky is a sure bet, so the anthers produce less than 100 pollen grains each. The most common plants that use closed pollination are cereals. In wheat, a few anthers do pop out into the sunlight after the grain has set. Why this happens is a mystery, but it's a bonus for forensic science and archaeology. One or two cereal pollen grains in a soil sample may tell the story of a crop of thousands.

How knowledge of the different types of pollination is used to interpret the significance of pollen assemblages, and how it will lead palynologists in many different directions in search of answers, is best illustrated by case histories rather than dry lists and descriptions.

Most forensic palynology cases involve the comparison of control samples with forensic samples to prove or disprove a relationship between them. For example, if a person is suspected of having committed a crime, the pollen assemblages from soil samples at the crime scene (control samples) will be compared with pollen collected from the suspect's possessions (forensic samples).

In most cases, a mixture of pollen types from wind- and animal-pollinated plants provides the incriminating or exonerating evidence. In Samantha Hall's case, only insect-pollinated plants provided the primary evidence. A case I worked on after Samantha Hall's case didn't fit either of these scenarios. It was pollen from a cleistogamous (closed flower) species in a single forensic sample that proved to be the downfall of a serial rapist.

Cereal Points to Serial Rapist

After I completed my PhD in late 1997 my daughters and I moved from Queensland back to Perth, Western Australia. Perth is my home town and my girls' birthplace but they had grown up in Queensland. It was a difficult move. We left behind the girls' kindergarten and school friends, and their friends' parents, who had been my support network for almost 13 years. The upside of the move was that in Perth we would be near my family, and the girls would have a few quality years with their terminally ill father, who had moved back to Perth several years beforehand.

Selling our beautiful home, farewelling friends, packing and planning our overland trip back to Perth were all-consuming. It wasn't until we arrived in Perth that reality struck. I was no longer a student—I needed a real job. In the climate of downsizing at the time there were no full-time jobs for palynologists. Eventually I found a part-time position databasing palynological data. It was soul-destroying work and not what I'd spent years completing a PhD for. Apart from applying for postdoctoral fellowships that wouldn't be available until the following year, I was stumped as to where to look next for work. Having had my first taste of success with Sam's case in Queensland, I decided to introduce forensic palynology to the WA Police Service.

Tim Atherton, a Queenslander who had recently been appointed an Assistant Police Commissioner with the WA Police Service and knew of my work in Queensland, arranged for me to give a presentation on forensic palynology to a select group of police. No longer having access to cheap university facilities, I spent a considerable amount of money having photographic and text slides commercially produced and hiring a slide projector in preparation for the presentation.

This was my big moment, a possible future career, but as my car nosed into a parking bay outside police headquarters I panicked. What was I doing here? Was I really going to walk into police headquarters and talk to police? Who the heck was I to be telling them what to do?...I was a recently graduated PhD student, the lowliest of the low in the academic world. Maybe I'd just go home...but then, my mother had been so proud of me as she waved me goodbye and wished me luck that morning. After a few deep breaths and thoughts about wasting the money I had spent preparing for the presentation, I braced myself and made it into the front foyer of the building.

Fumbling for the business card I'd paid too much to have made the day before, I confidently stated to the officer manning the reception desk: 'Dr Lynne Milne to see Assistant Commissioner Tim Atherton'.

This was the first time I'd used my new title in an official capacity. It felt sooooo good. The man at the desk immediately phoned to locate Tim. Wow, this Dr trick really works! My back straightened and my head reached for the ceiling. By the time an officer arrived to escort me to Tim's office I was in control.

Tim is a tall man, like many police I have since worked with, and he puts people at ease the moment he walks into a room. Congratulating me on my PhD thesis being accepted and joking about my new title, he led me into the room where my talk would be delivered. The tables and chairs were in no particular order, so we moved the tables to the side and placed the chairs in audience mode while we exchanged jokes about being Queenslanders.

Tim was due at a meeting shortly after my talk was to begin but he would stay to introduce me to my audience. I was thankful that he remained with me while they filed in, as almost every person who came through the door filled the door frame. The room and my confidence shrank accordingly. But oh joy, the odd female officer came through the door. If they could work with such large beings, so could I.

My talk went well and the audience was enthusiastic at question time.

'Would it be possible to extract pollen from a passport that has been flushed down an aeroplane toilet?' was the least attractive question. My considered reply was honest, but avoiding such a job was also on my mind.

'Possibly, but pollen from the waste products of more than one person would contaminate the sample', I suggested.

'Well, could you get pollen from a suitcase?' the officer continued. He was involved in tracing the origins of illegal immigrants who arrived by air without any form of identification.

'Yes, a suitcase could contain pollen from its country of origin', I replied. The next question would lead to my first forensic palynology case in Western Australia.

'Would a pair of shoes that have been stored for three years still have pollen on them?' asked another officer.

'Definitely. Pollen preserves for millions of years in favourable conditions. There could be thousands of pollen grains on the shoes', I answered.

'Would you be able to tell where the person who wore the shoes lived or worked?' the officer continued.

'It's unlikely that the pollen assemblage from the shoes would narrow down where the person lived to a specific locality, but it might provide information about the vegetation type the person is commonly associated with', I replied, hedging my bets with a negative and a positive.

I didn't hold much hope for a palynological resolution in this sort of case. Forensic palynology is quite simple when it involves the comparison of two or more samples, but trying to pinpoint where a single pollen assemblage may have come from is difficult. Some palynologists would decline the job. Nevertheless, after confirming that the shoes had been kept in a sealed exhibit bag since they had been collected, and that airborne pollen contamination was therefore not an issue, I agreed to meet with the officer concerned to learn more about the case.

Several days later I set out to meet Detective Sergeant John Leembruggen at the Sexual Assault Unit to learn more and decide whether palynology might be of use in helping to resolve the case. The address I had been given was in the centre of the city, where parking is at a premium. I looked for the building before deciding where to park. In my naivety I searched for a building with some indication that it was police premises—but saw none. After several passes in the general area and much searching and squinting to find the tiny street numbers, I eventually found it—a small faceless building with windows that were opaque from the outside. So what did I expect? WA Police Service Sexual Assault Unit emblazoned across the front? Dumbo!

John met me in reception and led me into a conference room. He explained that the shoes he hoped I might examine for pollen were from a serial rape case—Operation Web. This operation had been set up the previous year when evidence from DNA and victims' accounts had linked a number of assaults to one offender. The assaults had occurred over a period of five years. From identikit pictures constructed with help from the victims, the police knew that the rapist was of Aboriginal descent.

Covering most of a wall in the conference room was a large map of the Perth metropolitan area. Small coloured markers pinned to it indicated the places where assaults had taken place. They were randomly spread across the suburbs. This lack of pattern was puzzling. Most serial offenders carry out their criminal activities in areas close to their home or workplace and, from maps of these activities, forensic specialists can determine the most likely area in which an offender lives or works. Police at first believed that the rapist lived in the city. But with no pattern to his activities, did he use public transport? That he might be from the country had also been considered. Was he an itinerant worker in country areas who visited the city between jobs?

The shoes that police wished me to work on were found in a car the rapist had stolen in a northern suburb of Perth and driven to the eastern outskirts of the metropolitan area, where he entered a house and assaulted the woman who lived there. Leaving the scene after the assault he misjudged a corner, crashed the car and fled the scene. The shoes in the car didn't belong to the owners of the car, nor did they come from the victim's household. It was assumed they belonged to the rapist.

As I understood it, police had been visiting lock-ups and jails in both the country and the city on a regular basis, searching for an individual matching the description of the rapist and collecting DNA from likely suspects.

Western Australia covers an area of about 2.5 million square kilometres—about one-third the size of the total area of continental Australia—a huge area for police to search. Police also had to consider that the person they were searching for might have come from another State. It was like looking for the proverbial needle in a haystack. Could palynology narrow down the search area?

If I had taken the advice of certain colleagues I wouldn't have touched the case. A nil result was most likely and would put the discipline of palynology in a bad light—just when I was trying to promote it. Sensing my reticence, John suggested that even if the search area was halved, it would help their investigation. If that was the case, then yes, I'd be happy to give it a go.

The following week, with my briefcase newly fitted out with sterile instruments and containers and the obligatory disposable gloves, I returned to the Sexual Assault Unit building to work my magic on the shoes. Having never removed a pollen sample from shoes before I was hoping to be left alone to ponder what to do. It was not to be. All the occupants of the building wanted to know what was going on and a short version of my talk the previous week was requested.

Eventually, with the help of a female officer, Detective Senior Constable Kellie Properjohn, the scene was set to open the exhibit bag that held the shoes. The table was cleaned and covered with aluminium foil, and the instruments were lined up. The big moment had come: the shoes were laid out on the 'operating table'. To my horror, the soles of the shoes had very little soil or mud on them, just dust and bits of plant material in the tread. It wasn't looking good.

Kellie and I took one shoe each and brushed and scraped off what dust and dirt we could find on the soles of the shoes. Then, using sterile vegetable knives, we scraped out the material in the tread. Numerous fragments of straw were firmly lodged in discrete slits 3 millimetres deep that formed part of the tread in the soles of the shoes (Plate 5). Each piece of straw was exactly the same length as the slit it occupied, and so firmly lodged at the base of the slits that it took considerable time and effort to remove them. I didn't think the straw fragments themselves would be significant, but I thought they should be removed because pollen below them might be of interest.

Because of other commitments I wasn't able to work on the shoe sample immediately. As a novice forensic palynologist, it wasn't until the following week that it dawned on me that washing the soles of the shoes would remove pollen more firmly attached to the shoes than the pollen we'd scraped off or dug out onto the aluminium foil. With several large bottles of distilled water I returned to the Sexual Assault Unit, but forgot to take a container to wash the shoes in. All Kellie and I could find was a small plastic lunchbox. After much scrubbing of the lunch box and laughter we managed to wash the soles of the shoes in it, swearing each other to secrecy about our method and the container used.

Before chemically processing the two samples (the shoe scrapings and washings) to remove their mineral content, I examined the sample scraped from the soles of the shoes under a low-powered reflected light microscope, and had it photographed. The sample contained the usual grains of quartz sand, two gravel pebbles, insect remains, a small piece of animal bone and the many straw fragments (Plate 6). During the chemical processing all these larger fragments would be removed, so it was important to have a record of the complete sample.

To my surprise, the organic residues extracted from both of the samples contained many thousands of pollen grains, and the sample from the shoe washings was as rich in pollen as the sample brushed and scraped from the shoes. More than 80% of the pollen was from the gum tree family (Myrtaceae) and grasses. The remainder of the pollen types included she-oak, pine, daisy, banksia, saltbush and a few unidentifiable pollen types, including several very large grass-like pollen grains that were much larger than any grass pollen I had seen before. Grass pollen is circular and has a single circular pore.

The total pollen assemblage suggested a eucalypt woodland vegetation that occurs in country areas close to Perth and the south-western part of the State, and is typical of urban golf courses, parks and the area in which the assault, when the shoes were left behind, occurred. The rarity of some types of pollen suggested that the person who wore the shoes didn't come from an area near the coast, or from the more arid areas north and east of Perth. As I had thought from the start, it wasn't possible to link the pollen assemblage to a precise location but I had eliminated more than half of the State, as requested.

My meeting with John to report the findings was tense. More to the point, I was tense. On the drive to the city it had occurred to me that although my findings reduced the search area, the target population was decreased only minimally. Western Australia's population is concentrated in the south-western part of the State.

After I reported the results of my pollen analysis and its limitations to John, he shifted uneasily in his chair, then sat deep in thought. Sensing disappointment and frustration rising within him, I sat mute, like a naughty child waiting for a parent to explode and mete out punishment. But of course this wasn't aimed at me. John passionately wanted this case to be resolved, and he was happy with any information, no matter how small, that palynology might provide. However, he didn't know what to expect from it, or how my results might be further interpreted. Taking a deep breath, and using the table as an imaginery map of the State and his forefinger as a pointer, he questioned me in an effort to get a better understanding of the meaning of my results.

'Can you tell me if he's from the country or the city?' Point, point, but no answer from me.

'If he's from the country, which town is he from?' The finger moved over the imaginery map rapidly. I watched, mesmerised and still mute. This was my first Perth case, my first opportunity to demonstrate that palynology was an invaluable forensic tool. Instead, it felt like I was on trial and my credibility, and that of palynology, was being examined. But John was just doing his job. Asking pertinent questions. Me? I was reacting to this like some members of the public when they're 'questioned' by the police. Defensively.

'Could he be from the north, south or east of the city?' John asked. The imaginary map on the table was now of the Perth metropolitan area, and his finger moved across it in three of the four cardinal directions.

'Can you tell me if he is from Midland or Fremantle?' Still I was mute. John's hand rose slowly, then fell to the table as he sat back in his chair.

'Isn't there anything more you can tell me?' he implored.

Now it was my turn, but where was my voice? 'Well...There are a couple of things I'd like to investigate further, but it'll take quite a bit more time', I squeaked. He sat forward.

'What do you have in mind?' he queried, raising his eyebrows. I took a deep breath and began to feel more like myself.

'I'm puzzled about the amount of straw in the shoes, and I've been wondering why it was so firmly stuck in the bottom of the tread,' I continued, grasping at the proverbial straw. He nodded, urging me to continue.

'There are also a few large pollen grains I can't identify, and I suspect they may be related to the straw.' I was referring to the large grass-like pollen I had not been able to identify.

John nodded again for me to continue. 'I didn't investigate these things before I came to see you because you said you have literally no budget for me to work on the case. I thought it best to give you the opportunity to decide if you wanted me to proceed further', I explained. Phew, I'd got out of that one, but it was the truth.

We finally agreed that I would investigate the straw mystery further, but still with little remuneration.

For the straw fragments to lodge horizontally in the base of the slits on the soles of the shoes, and fit into them precisely, I assumed that the person wearing the shoes must have walked over brittle vegetation. I couldn't think of any other plausible explanation. Surely someone wouldn't have painstakingly cut the straw fragments to size and pushed them into the slits!

Having grown up on a wheat and sheep farm I had painful memories of walking barefoot over stubble, the short stalks left in the ground after cereal crops have been cut for hay. The memory of falling off onto stubble from a motorbike I was forbidden to ride was even more painful. Could the rapist have walked over stubble left from hay cutting? Yes, but would walking on wild oats or other weed stubble produce the same result? Then there was the pollen. If the rapist walked over wheat stubble, might the large grass-like pollen grains be from wheat? After all, wheat is a grass.

Wheat and wild oats are cleistogamous—their flowers don't open and they produce very little pollen. I had already described the large grass-like pollen found in the shoe pollen assemblage to a colleague and asked him if it might be cereal pollen. He thought it unlikely, as he'd not come across any during his work on contemporary and young sediments in country areas of Western Australia. So much for wheat pollen. I was left holding the straw. Was it from wild oats or a cereal crop?

Our dog had more than his usual number of walks that week. We tramped through spare blocks, along unkempt verges and ventured into sad gardens. No matter what shoes I wore, how hard I tramped, or how dry the wild oats were, the soles of my shoes remained straw free. Wild oats weren't the culprit. It was time to ask a few farmers some questions.

Most of my cousins and my two stepbrothers are farmers. A phone call to my favourite farmer cousin and one stepbrother confirmed my suspicions. The tread of their working boots collected a few straw fragments after they walked over stubble; and stubble could even penetrate thin rubber soles.

I was still puzzled about the amount of straw in the rapist's shoes. Every possible part of the tread contained a fragment, but my farmer informants insisted that their shoes only collected a few pieces of straw.

'How would someone get straw in *all* of the separate slits in a pair of shoes?' I asked my cousin Grant.

'They'd have to walk over a lot of stubble', Grant said in his usual cheeky manner.

'Yeah right, I know *that*', I replied, acknowledging his cheek. 'But why would someone spend most of their time walking over stubble?'

'Mmmm', he thought for a second. 'Someone who worked on a chaff-cutting farm?' he suggested.

Now that was a thought. Chaff, chopped-up hay and straw. The crop was cut while it was still green. That meant the pollen inside the wheat head might be found in chaff.

'Are there farms that just grow hay for cutting into chaff?' I questioned.

'Yep', Grant replied. He's a man of few words except when telling jokes.

'Do you know any chaff farmers?' I asked.

'Nope.'

'Well, have you any suggestions as to where I might find one?' I persisted.

'You could try around York or Northam', he suggested.

York and Northam are about an hour's drive east and north-east respectively of the Perth metropolitan area. My stepbrothers' farms were in the Northam area. I was in luck, but first I should find out what wheat pollen looked like. If the large grass-like grains found on the shoes were wheat pollen, it would provide enough evidence for me to suggest that the rapist could have been involved in the chaff-cutting industry.

Getting samples of wheat heads would be no problem. My family could provide them. But I'm no biologist or botanist, and the anatomy of the reproductive parts of grass plants was a mystery to me. My attempts to find pollen in wild oats had been fruitless. I needed to find someone who knew what the anthers of wheat looked like and where they were in the plants. A phone call to the Department of Agriculture led me to their experimental grain crops and a man as passionate about the different varieties of wheat that he was growing as I am about pollen. It was late October and the wheat grains had already set, so finding plants willing to reveal their pollen was not easy.

We walked between the rows of experimental wheat crops choosing likely plants. With a fine pair of tweezers my companion peeled back several layers of fine tissue inside the husk and on the side of the immature wheat grain, and there it was—sometimes. I collected several samples to compare with pollen in the shoe samples, and once again phoned my stepbrother, my cousin Grant and his sister Julie to ask them to collect soil and wheat heads from their crops. I would use the wheat heads to collect pollen from the different varieties of wheat for comparison, and document the pollen assemblages in the soils for comparison with the soil pollen assemblage from the rapist's shoes. My relatives were very efficient and the samples arrived promptly in the mail.

I was right—the wheat pollen and the large grass-like pollen in the shoe pollen assemblage were literally identical. What's more, the soil pollen assemblage from the York–Northam area was most similar to that on the shoes. The evidence was looking good. But for it to fit into the time frame of the assault I still needed to talk to a chaff-cutting farmer to find out when the hay was cut, when it was cut into chaff and who was employed to do it.

Again I was in luck. One of the largest chaff-cutting farms in the area was next door to the farm of one of my stepbrothers. Eddie, the chaff-cutting farmer, was very helpful and provided me with all the information I needed. Chaff-cutting farmers employ teams of itinerant workers. During the period from mid-October to mid-November, 10–20 people are employed on each farm to stook the hay after it is cut, and a handful of these workers return from December through to February to cut the hay into chaff.

Eddie's information fitted well with my theory. The assault in question occurred in early March, shortly after the chaff-cutting season had finished. The teams of workers employed by the chaff-cutting farmers were mostly Aboriginal.

My final report submitted in December of that year concluded that: the person who wore the shoes had recently walked in an area supporting a eucalypt woodland vegetation, had walked for a considerable period of time over stubble and could be associated with the hay/chaff-cutting industry. The report also included a list of names and phone numbers of prominent chaff-cutting farmers in the York–Northam area and one further north in Geraldton. There was no more finger-pointing on imaginary maps from John, just a broad grin.

On a balmy January night several weeks after my report had been submitted, I sat in a friend's garden sipping champagne, as we are wont to do on such nights. Our daughters were inside watching television and a late news summary had interrupted their programme. My youngest came rushing out excitedly.

'Mum, Mum, they've caught your rapist.' My friends were stunned. I'd been raped?

That night sleep didn't come easily. I tossed and turned, wondering if my work had led police to the rapist or if I'd been totally off the track and they'd found him some other way. Perhaps he was a butcher from another country town, worked on the wharves or was a fisherman?

The important thing was that they had found him. At work early the next morning I phoned an excited John to congratulate him and the rest of the team, and tentatively ask if palynology had been of help.

'What do you mean? Of course it was. You said go to Northam, so we did', came the buoyant reply.

It's not my place here to describe how police chanced upon the now convicted rapist, or discuss other forensic methods that were used in conjunction with the evidence from palynology, but I can tell you that they visited Eddie the chaff-cutting farmer.

A Microscopic World

The success of pollen analysis in the Samantha Hall case depended on my ability to distinguish between pollen from different species of wattle (*Acacia*). Had I been rash in so readily agreeing that this could be done? Possibly. I knew little of wattle pollen morphology. On the other hand, my eye for the finer details of pollen morphology had been well honed during the last few years. My PhD thesis was based on pollen morphology and I was fascinated with the symmetry and structure of pollen and its stunning surface patterns.

To the untrained eye it's often difficult to distinguish one animal or plant species from another similar species. All elephants have trunks, monkeys have long tails and a rose is a rose. It's the finer structural details of a living organism that identify it to the smallest unit of classification, the species. Reproductive structures, including pollen, are important characteristics in plant classification.

Pollen grains come in an incredible range of shapes and sizes, and with wondrous surface patterns. They are one of nature's masterpieces and, in a forensic sense, they are botanical fingerprints. What more could a forensic scientist want than a microscopic tool that is produced in vast numbers, can be identified to a particular plant type and is exceptionally resistant to decay? Despite precautions, criminals may leave or take away from a crime scene lots of something so small they can't see it. And pollen's resistance to decay means that it can still incriminate them years after a crime was committed.

Before elaborating on the physical wonders of pollen and the characteristics used to identify it to a particular plant group or species, some background information on taxonomy—that is, the way organisms, both animal and vegetable, are classified—will be useful for those not biologically inclined.

Classification involves the grouping together of living things according to the characteristics they share. These groups are organised into categories. Each category belongs to a higher ranked category and, in turn, this higher ranked category belongs to a still higher one. In this way the classification system used for both animals and plants forms a pyramid-like structure.

How plants are classified is governed by the International Code of Botanical Nomenclature (ICBN), a rule book of dos and don'ts. It designates the rank of kingdom at the top of the pyramid, descending through the ranks of phylum, class, order, family, genus and eventually to the basic unit, the species, at the bottom of the pyramid (see diagram below). There may be midway groups such as subclasses or suborders, and a family may have subfamilies within which there are tribes and subtribes.

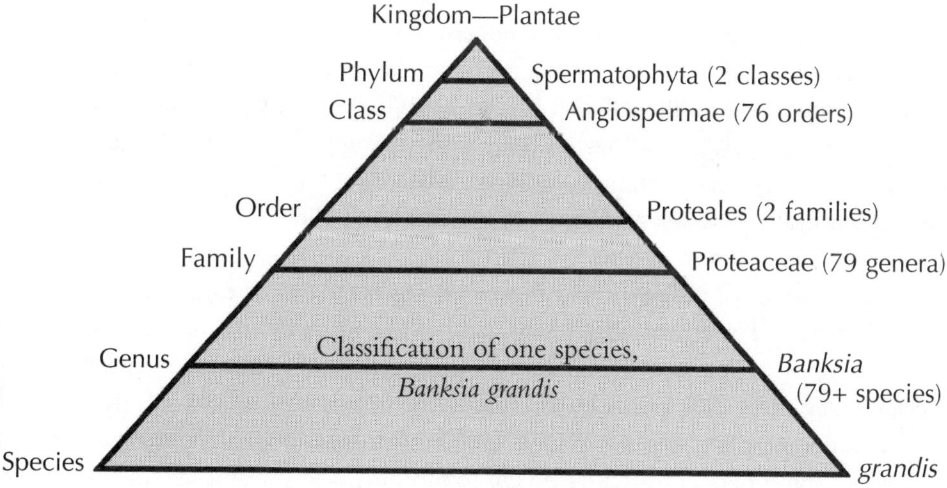

The plant kingdom and its subgroups. *Classification of one species,* Banksia grandis, *illustrating the major hierarchies in the classification system and the published number of subgroups in each group. Note that the number of divisions in any one hierarchy (e.g. species in a genus) is subject to change as more is learnt of the plant world.*

A species is a group of individuals that are more or less identical and can interbreed. Species that are closely related are grouped together into a genus, the classification rank above species. Each species is identified by two names. The first is the actual genus the species belongs to, and the second is specific only to that species. The genus and species names are always typed in italics, or underlined if written by hand. The genus name starts with a capital letter and the species name with a lower case letter. All wattles belong to the genus *Acacia*, but *Acacia falcata* is a species of *Acacia*. This system of naming organisms was established by the eighteenth-century Swedish naturalist Carl von Linné, and is called the Linnean System of Binomial Nomenclature.

Conventionally, if the same species or a different species of the same genus is mentioned in the same paragraph more than once, only the first letter of the genus is written the second and subsequent times it is referred to as long as another genus hasn't been referred to in between the first and last reference, and the genus is not at the beginning of a sentence. For example: '*Acacia sophorae* and *A. saligna* occur at Noosa'. Here endeth the lesson.

The definition of pollen in the *Australian Pocket Oxford Dictionary* is 'fertilising powder discharged from flowers' anthers'. When we were children, we put our fingers into the centre of flowers to collect the yellow dust. We also saw bees flitting from flower to flower with yellow legs. This powdery stuff called pollen looked the same in every flower. I doubt whether any of us asked if different-looking flowers make different-looking pollen. Even if we had, the answer would probably have been no because the study of pollen is not a science that many lay people know about.

When a mass of pollen from a flower of one plant type is examined under a high-powered microscope, the mass can be seen to be thousands of identical pollen grains. Pollen grains from another plant type will all also be identical to each other...but different from the pollen of the first plant. So yes, flowers from different plant types produce different-looking pollen. It is this that enables palynologists to identify pollen found in soil or on objects down to a particular plant type, or even a specific plant.

The major characteristics used to describe pollen are its overall size and shape, and the type and size of its surface ornamentation, wall structure and openings from which the male sex cells emerge. As a general rule, pollen grains produced by all species from a single genus have similar geometric shapes and similar types of openings and surface ornamentation, but the pollen of each species will differ within these parameters. However, nature likes to leave us with a few challenges, so there are a few exceptions to these rules.

With apologies to the men of this world, palynologists are not interested in the male sex cells. The cytoplasm and its male nuclei (the contents of the pollen grain) are chemically removed from pollen before pollen analysis; what remains is the outer skeleton that protects the male cells on their journey in search of a mate. It is the structure of this skeleton that varies among species and can help solve crimes. To appreciate how pollen is used to solve crimes, it helps to know what it looks like and understand how the different structures are related to the sex life of plants.

Pollen is very very small. It even looks small when it's magnified to several hundred times its normal size. Pollen grains range in size from about 5 to 200 μm (micrometres, or microns for short) in diameter, but most are between 10 and 70 μm. There are 1000 μm in a millimetre and 10 000 μm in a centimetre. These numbers mean little until they are put into the context of 'our world'. If pollen grains with a diameter of 10 μm were placed end to end in a line it would take 100 grains to create a line 1 millimetre long, and 1000 grains to make a line 1 centimetre long.

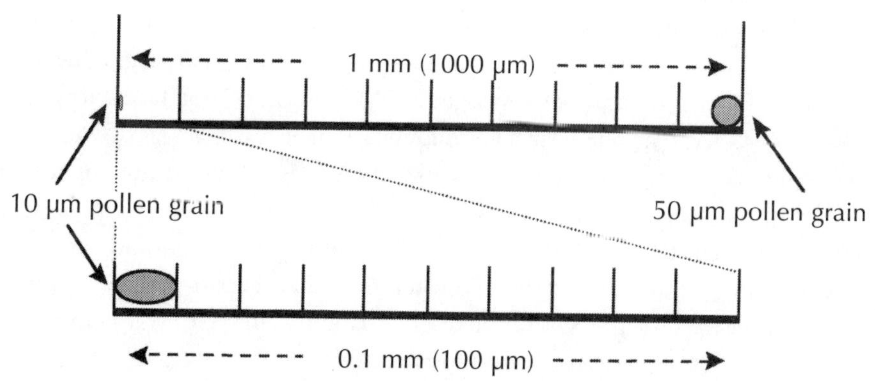

The size of pollen grains relative to 1 millimetre. *Pollen grains range in size from 5 to 200 μm in diameter, but most fall within the 10–70 μm range.*

'Pollen belongs to a world of another size'[2]—a microscopic world. A palynologist's tool of trade is a transmitted light microscope that magnifies pollen up to x 1000. Pollen is sandwiched between a glass microscope slide and a thin glass cover slip and placed on the microscope stage. A light at the base of the microscope shines up through the slide. Pollen is viewed by looking down the eye pieces above the slide.

To examine the fine surface detail of pollen at much higher magnifications, a scanning electron microscope (SEM) is used; and to magnify the structural detail of pollen walls the grains are sliced very finely with a tiny diamond knife, and the resulting thin sections are viewed in a transmission electron microscope (TEM). Plate 7 illustrates a single pollen grain photographed with light and scanning and transmission electron microscopy. This is a fossil Proteaceae pollen grain, *Proteacidites carobelindiae*, named after my daughters.

Photography is another tool palynologists need. Photos taken down a microscope—called photomicrographs—provide a permanent record of the size, shape, sculpture and other structural features of pollen from different species. Profiles of pollen in scientific journals consist of a written description and several photographs. To identify a dispersed pollen grain (e.g. one in soil), we refer to descriptions and photographs in scientific journals, our own pollen reference collections and now, our colleagues' websites. Cynical geologists, like my former husband, call palynologists stamp collectors. We collect photomicrographs.

In the 'olden days', before digital imaging, a darkroom for processing film and printing photos, and the skills to do so, were essential for palynologists. I developed and printed the photos for my doctoral thesis, some of which are reproduced here. Being strapped for cash at the time, I took advantage of the sculptural beauty of my subjects and my newly acquired photographic skills. Family and friends received enlarged SEM photos of my favourite pollen grains for Christmas one year. The following year it was black and white photos of my daughters, taken by a colleague and processed and printed by me and the girls. That year, Caroline fell asleep in the darkroom, while Belinda struggled alone with the developing trays. In later years Caroline would become so adept in the darkroom that she could tell me what filter or light exposure to use to improve a print. Nothing like child labour. They enjoyed helping, and in a sense my thesis was as much theirs as it was mine.

The universal comment from students when they first look down a microscope at pollen is – 'they all look the same'. Later they describe them by their shape, the one that looks 'like a golf ball' or 'like a football'. While helping develop photographs for my Honours thesis, my mother's most creative comparison of a pollen grain with an everyday object was 'the one that looks like a pair of panties, dear'. I can't remember what type of pollen grain it was, but because pollen is more or less symmetrical I suspect she was referring to knickers with leg holes as wide as the waist hole!

Pollen grains are usually bilaterally symmetrical and can be circular, oval, triangular, pentagonal or hexagonal (see diagram page 61), but with many variations on these and other geometrical themes. Circular grains may be spherical or disc-shaped; and triangular grains vary from a typical equilateral triangle with straight sides to those with varying degrees of concave or convex sides. The football shape, as in Australian Rules footballs, is elliptical, but again with many variations—from 'fat footballs' to 'long skinny footballs'. Plates 8 and 9 show a range of different pollen shapes.

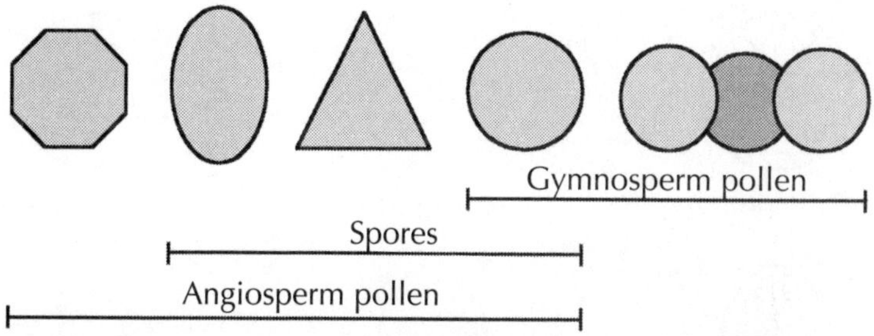

Examples of pollen and spore shapes*. The external outlines of pollen and spores are variations on basic geometric shapes. The general shape is always consistent within a species and often within a genus, but may vary within a family.*

Most pollen grains have openings, called apertures, from which the male sex cells escape when a grain lands on a friendly stigma. Apertures may be circular 'pores', or slits called 'colpi' (sing. colpus), or a combination of pores and colpi (see diagram page 62). Each aperture type has a name. For example, pollen with two pores is termed biporate; pollen with three pores and three colpi is called tricolporate. Some thin-walled pollen has no defined apertures, but rather its wall ruptures to release the male sex cells.

The ornamentation or patterning on the surface of pollen grains is termed 'sculpture'. This may be regularly spaced or consist of random depressions or holes on the outer wall, or protruding elements. Each sculptural type has a name. Examples include echinate (with spines), baculate (with rod-like elements), verrucate (with hemispherical elements) and reticulate (network-like) (see diagram page 63). The shape and size of these sculptural elements varies on different species. Some pollen has two different elements, such as spines and rods, or even a combination of small holes and a protrusive element. The general sculptural type of pollen is usually visible in light microscopy. Some of the different pollen sculpture types can be seen in Plates 8 and 9.

Scanning electron microscopy (SEM) is used to see the finer sculptural details (Plate 9). Some of these intricate patterns are works of art. One of my SEM photographs of the surface of a Proteaceae pollen grain was recently enlarged and included in an art exhibition (Plate 10). The actual area the photo

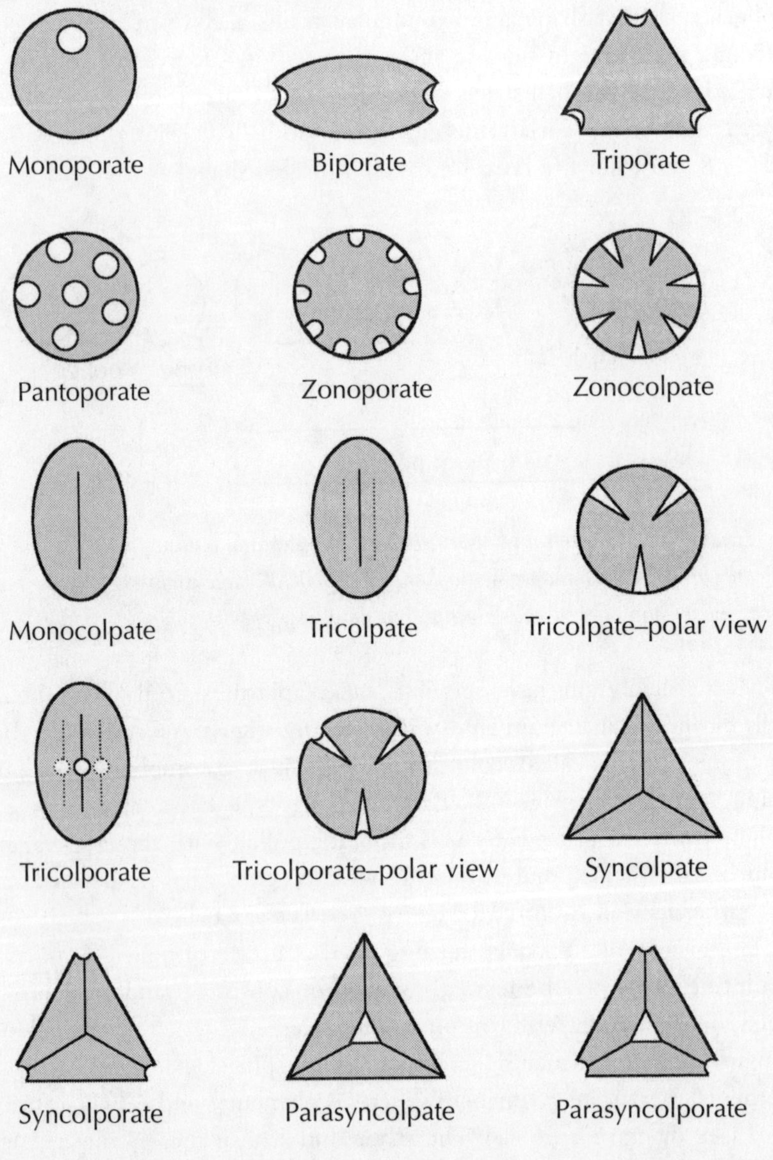

Examples of pollen apertures. *Male sex cells emerge from the apertures in a pollen grain when it alights on a receptive stigma. These openings may be pores (circular or elliptical holes), colpi (slits) or a combination of pores and colpi. Each aperture configuration has its own terminology. All pollen from the same species (and often genus) has the same aperture type, but it may vary within a family.*

covers here is only about 5.5 µm by 4.5 µm. Less successful was one entered in an electron microscopy competition at a conference. It was entitled 'Moon Conference', as a play on the word conference and the act of 'mooning'—as in showing one's naked rear end. With a little imagination several 'rear ends' and a 'naked lady' standing sideways can be seen in the photo (Plate 11).

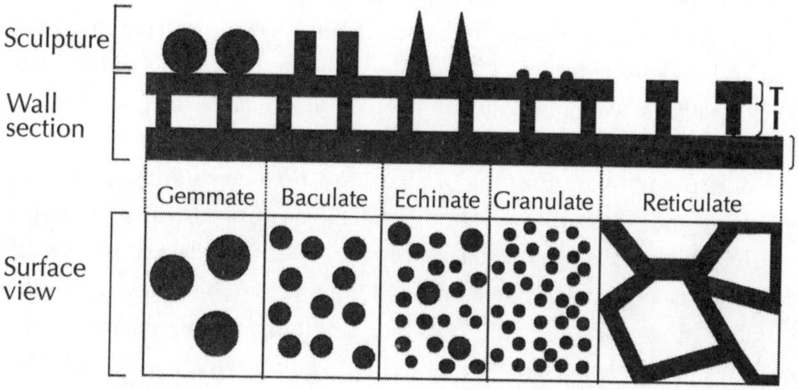

Examples of pollen wall structure and surface sculpture. *The most common wall layers of pollen that can be seen in the light microscope are the tectum (T), infratectum or columellate layer (I) and the foot layer (F). Pollen sculpture, the surface ornamentation, may be sculptural elements supported by the tectum or formed by depressions or holes in the tectum. The relative thickness of the wall layers and sculptural types are the same for all pollen from the same species.*

Pollen sculpture type is related to the method of dispersal. Most insect-pollinated plants (which include wattles) produce highly ornamented pollen to help them attach to pollinators. Pollen from wind-pollinated plants is usually quite light compared with the heavy pollen from insect-pollinated plants. It may have relatively thin walls and little ornamentation; be disc or torpedo shaped to increase its aerodynamic properties; or have bladders or sacs to keep it aloft.

Grass is wind pollinated and the surface of its pollen appears smooth or slightly grainy in light microscopy, but in SEM it can be seen that its surface ornamentation consists of granulate-like bodies. Some wind-pollinated plants, like the Antarctic or Southern Beech (*Nothofagus*), have highly ornamented pollen like the pollen of animal-pollinated plants, and use other physical characteristics to make them more aerodynamic. *Nothofagus* pollen looks like a prickly frisbee—a disc covered with spines (Plate 9A and B).

Pollen walls are predominantly composed of a tough, acid-resistant biopolymer called sporopollenin. After pollen is shed from an anther, the material inside it (cytoplasm and the male sex cells) will decay relatively quickly if it's exposed to the elements, but the pollen wall may survive normal weathering processes for many years in soil or on objects exposed to the atmosphere. However, if pollen is not exposed to alternate wet and dry conditions in the presence of oxygen over the years, and it is either kept in a dry environment or is buried, it can survive for millions of years. For example, it can be found on objects collected from crimes many years ago, herbarium plant specimens dried hundreds of years ago and in sedimentary rocks deposited millions of years ago. This durability makes pollen an exceptionally useful tool in sciences such as geology, palaeontology, geography and archaeology and, of course, forensic science.

Pollen wall structure is another major characteristic used to differentiate the pollen of one species from that of another species. The walls of fresh pollen may have four discrete layers, but usually only the outer three layers survive the chemical processes pollen is subjected to before it can be microscopically analysed. Pollen walls sliced at 90° look like a colonnade (see diagram page 63). A solid base layer supports a row of columns upon which another decorative or solid layer rests. The base layer or inner wall of pollen is called a foot layer (or nexine) and the top or outer layer is the tectum. The layer of columns that connect the foot layer to the tectum is the'infratectum. The width of these layers relative to each other often helps identify which species pollen is from.

Palynology has its own descriptive language, or terminology. The morphology of pollen is so varied that this terminology is constantly increasing as palynologists study pollen groups not previously studied. Pollen from only a few of the world's plant species has been formally described.

In a soil sample there will be many, perhaps hundreds, of different types of pollen. Many of these may not have been described before. Unknown species are given a temporary name or an identity code—such as C1, for circular grain 1—and their general characteristics noted beside a sketch or photograph. This is often sufficient for comparison with pollen in other samples. This is easy forensic palynology. If the soil is from a known locality and it's necessary to know exactly what species the pollen is from, a botanist will identify plants at the site. Pollen is then collected from the actual plants (if they are flowering) and from herbarium specimens, to compare with pollen found in the soil sample. This is slightly more complicated forensic palynology. Stressful forensic palynology is when the pollen morphology of one species must be confidently distinguished from the morphology of pollen from numerous other species of the same genus. This was my challenge with wattle pollen and the murder of Samantha Hall.

Plate 1 The small cross that, until recently, stood near where Samantha's body was found in Noosa Woods in August 1996. This photograph was taken in 2003. The cross was stolen in early 2004. At the time of the murder this area was densely populated with flowering wattle shrubs.

Plate 2 The parking bay that the murderer allegedly backed into. It is thought that the victim was in the front passenger seat. At the time of the murder a solid bank of flowering wattles, like those illustrated in Plate 4, grew between the posts and along the side of the parking bay. A solitary young wattle shrub was growing there in August 2003 when this photograph was taken (inset).

Plate 3 Samantha Jane Hall at 23, in 1992.

Plate 4 Coastal wattles (*Acacia sophorae*) in Noosa Woods. In 1996 a similar bank of these plants lined the side of the parking bay where the murderer allegedly parked to remove Samantha's body from the car (see Plate 2).

Plate 5 The sole of the rapist's shoe, showing discrete slits in the black areas where the brittle pieces of straw were firmly lodged. This photograph was taken several weeks after the soles of the shoes had been washed. The small amount of debris seen here on the shoes came from material left in the bag they were stored in.

Plate 6 (inset) Material brushed and scraped from the soles of the rapist's shoes, spread across a 3-centimetre grid. Note the small pieces of straw.

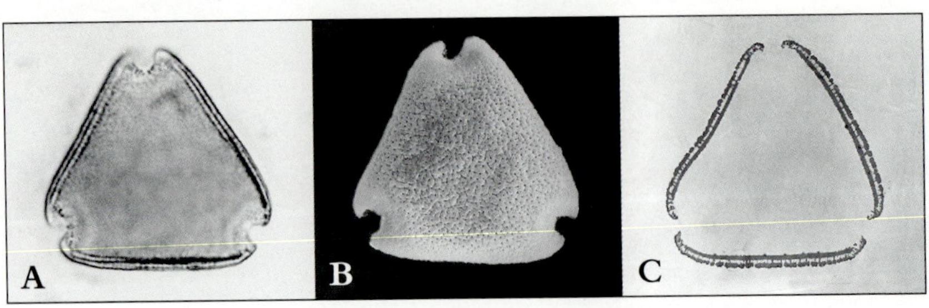

Plate 7 Light (A), scanning electron (B) and transmission electron (C) microscopy photographs of a single fossil pollen grain, *Proteacidites carobelindiae*, a relative of the modern Proteaceae (e.g. grevilleas and hakeas) genus *Petrophile*. Magnification x 900.

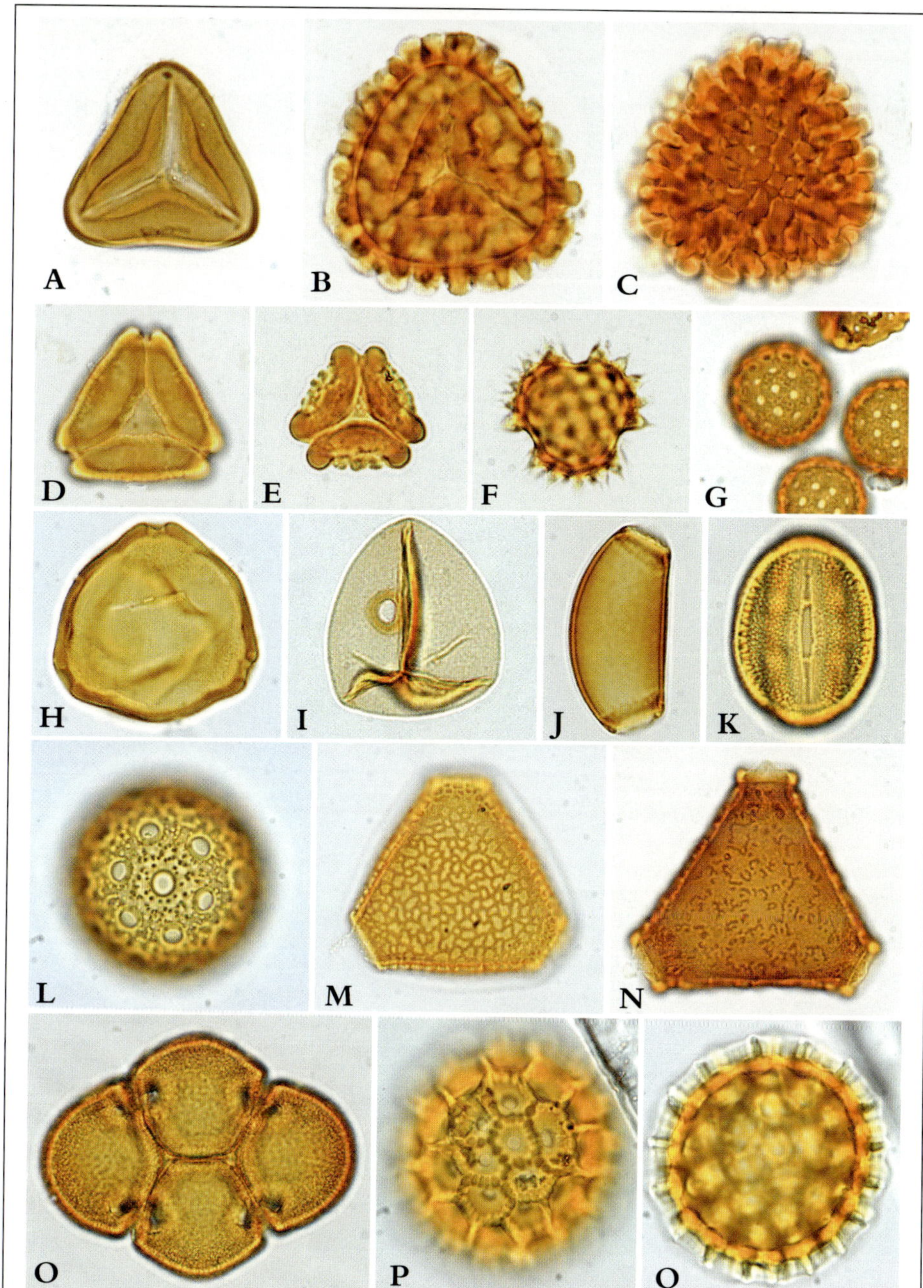

Plate 8 Processed spores (A–C) and pollen grains (D–Q) photographed in their natural colour in a light microscope. **A.** *Cyathea* (tree fern); **B, C.** *Polypodium* (fern), views of both sides of spore; **D, E.** Two different Myrtaceae pollen grains (e.g. gum trees and bottle-brushes): D. *Eucalyptus gomphocephala* (Tuart), E. Myrtaceae sp. from rapist's shoes; **F.** *Olearia rudis* (Azure Daisy Bush); **G.** *Atriplex* sp. (saltbush); **H.** *Casuarina stricta* (She-oak); **I.** *Erharta longiflora* (Annual Veldt Grass); **J.** *Dryandra sessilis* (Parrot Bush); **K.** *Euphorbia terracina* (Geraldton Carnation); **L.** *Ptilotus exaltatus* (Tall Mulla Mulla); **M.** *Symphionema paludosum;* **N.** *Grevillea robusta* (Silky Oak); **O.** Tetrad (four grains) of *Leschenaultia linarioides*; **P, Q.** *Tribulus platypterus* (Fish Poison): P. surface view showing reticulate (network-like) sculpture and circular pores, Q. view through the centre of the grain showing the wall structure. Magnification x 500–900.

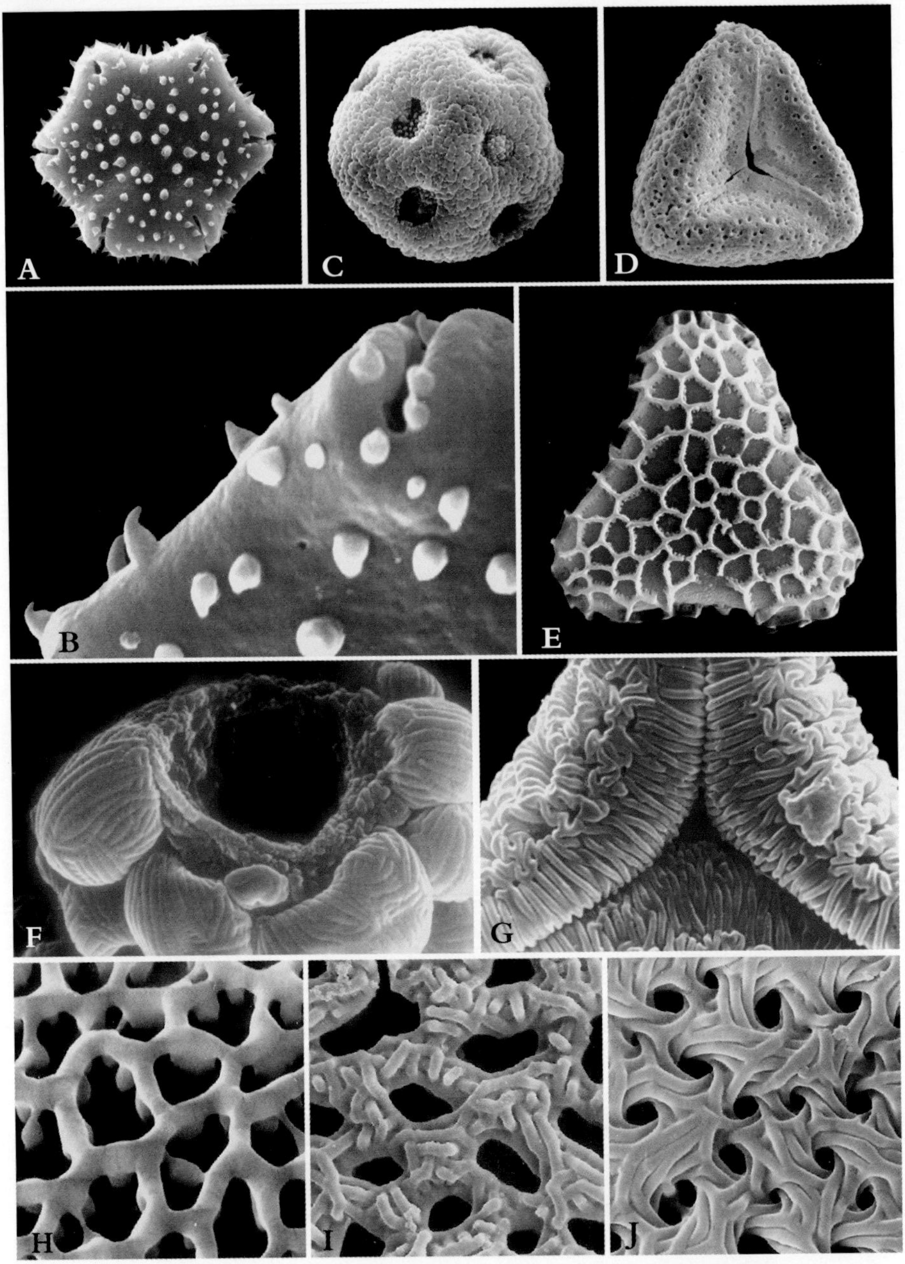

Plate 9 Scanning electron microscope photographs of fossil pollen around 40 million years old (A–G) and reticulate surface sculpture of modern pollen (H–J). This type of photograph shows much finer sculptural detail than the light microscope photographs in Plate 8. **A, B.** Southern Beech (*Nothofagus*): A. whole grain, B. high magnification of slit-like pore and spiny sculpture; **C.** ?Trimeniaceae; **D.** Myrtaceae (e.g. gum trees and bottlebrushes) has three colpi (slits) and pores (obscured) on the apices of the triangle; **E.** Proteaceae (e.g. grevilleas and hakeas) with reticulate sculpture; **F.** Pore of Proteaceae pollen with striate verrucate (hemispherical elements) sculpture; **G.** ?Loranthaceae, part grain showing intricate sculpture at the junction of the colpi (slits). Magnification A, C, D, E x 900–1600; B, F, G, H, I, J x 5000–11 000.

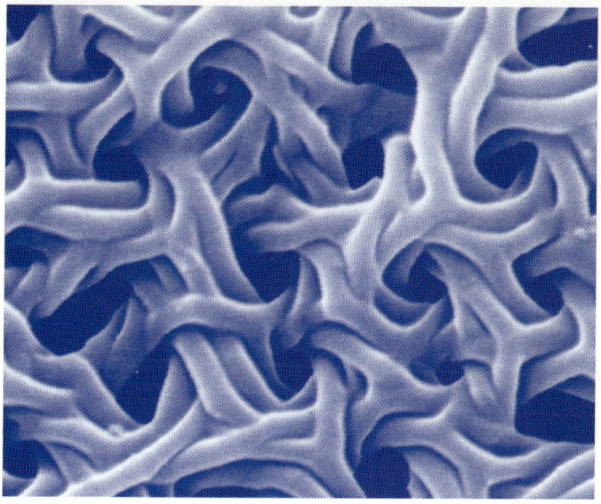

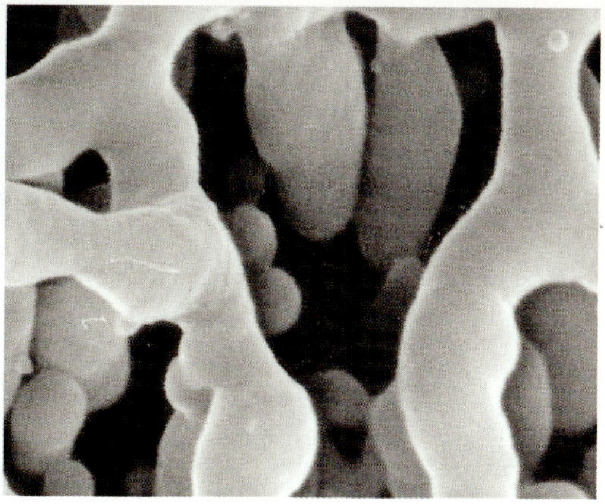

Plate 10 (left) A colour-enhanced scanning electron microscope photograph of the reticulate surface sculpture of *Petrophile ericifolia* (Proteaceae) pollen. An enlarged version of this was shown in an art exhibition. The photo is approximately 5.5 μm x 4.5 μm (magnified x 12 500).

Plate 11 (right) 'Moon Conference'. A scanning electron microscope photograph of the reticulate surface sculpture of *Petrophile circinata* (Proteaceae) pollen. With a little imagination several rear ends and a naked lady can be seen. The photo is 6.5 μm x 5 μm (magnified x 11 000).

Plate 12 (left) Elongated 'spike' inflorescences of *Acacia leiocalyx*, with worm.
Plate 13 (right) Spherical inflorescences of *Acacia saligna*.

A

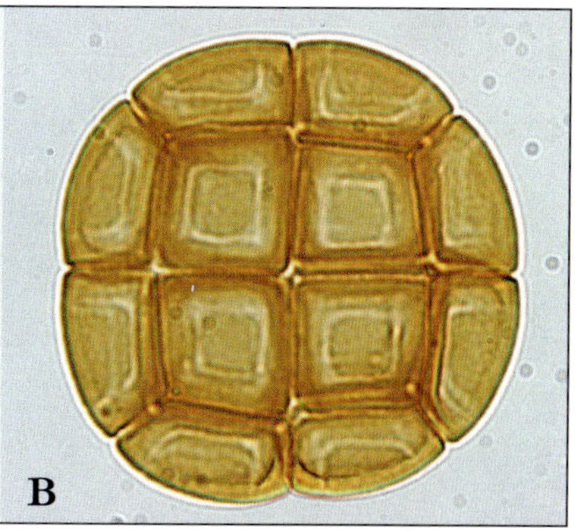

B

Plate 14 Light microscope photographs of *Acacia* pollen showing the different number and arrangement of the single pollen grains (monads) in the composite grains (polyads).
A. *Acacia pulchella*, with 12 monads and patterning on the surface of the monads;
B. *Acacia iteaphylla*, with 16 monads and square-like furrows on the surface of the monads. Magnification x 1100.

Plate 15 The author (left) with a colleague in the Hydrofluoric Acid Laboratory (School of Earth and Geographical Sciences, University of Western Australia). The box-like machine is a centrifuge used to spin samples in tubes, like those being held by the author, to concentrate the solid material. Note the protective overalls, gloves and visors. Photograph: David Haig.

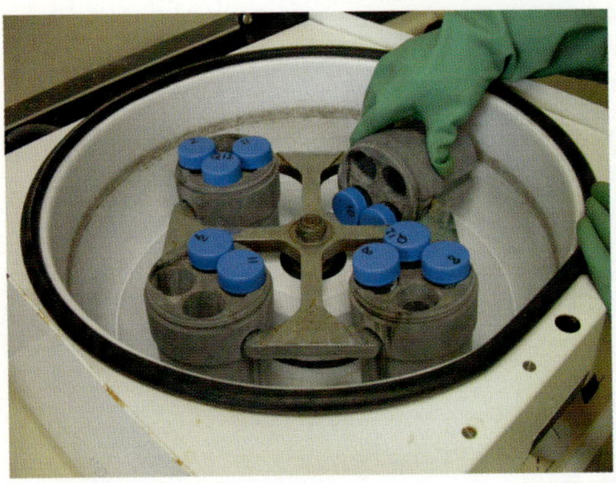

Plate 16 (left) A stationary centrifuge with tubes in the buckets, and one bucket being held horizontal to show their position when the machine spins the buckets. Photograph: David Haig.

Plate 17 (right) The centrifuge in action. Buckets containing the tubes are almost horizontal. Photograph: David Haig.

Plate 18 The car air filter after it was pulled apart to remove some of the cardboard filter for pollen analysis.

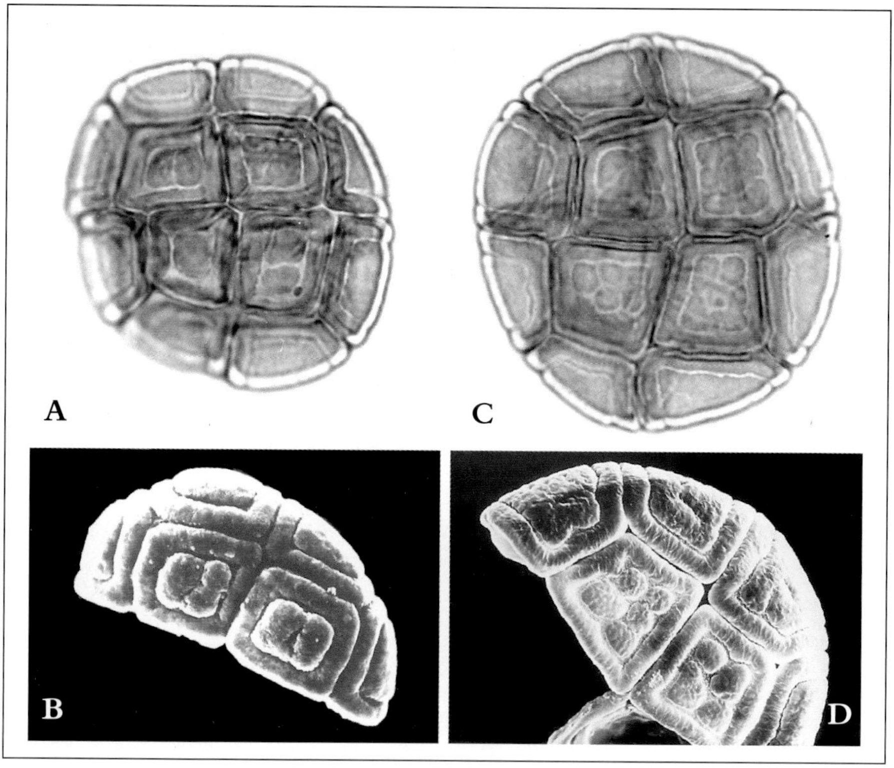

Plate 19 The original photographs of pollen from plant samples collected by police from the Noosa crime scene. Black and white light microscope photographs (**A, C**) of whole grains and scanning electron microscope photographs (**B, D**) of part grains. **A, B.** *Acacia sophorae* has the tectal 'islands' divided into two pillow-like structures; **C, D.** *Acacia saligna* has tectal islands divided four to six times. Magnification x 1200.

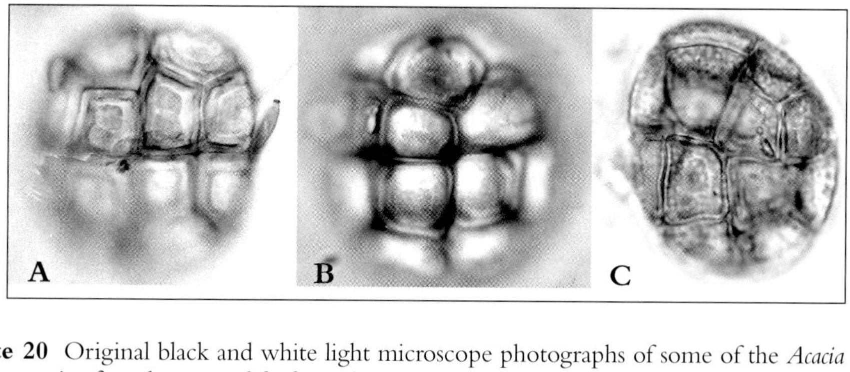

Plate 20 Original black and white light microscope photographs of some of the *Acacia* pollen grains found on tape-lifts from the suspect's clothing. Photographed unprocessed from temporary water-mounted slides. **A, B.** *Acacia sophorae*; **C.** Grain with small tectal islands. Magnification x 1000.

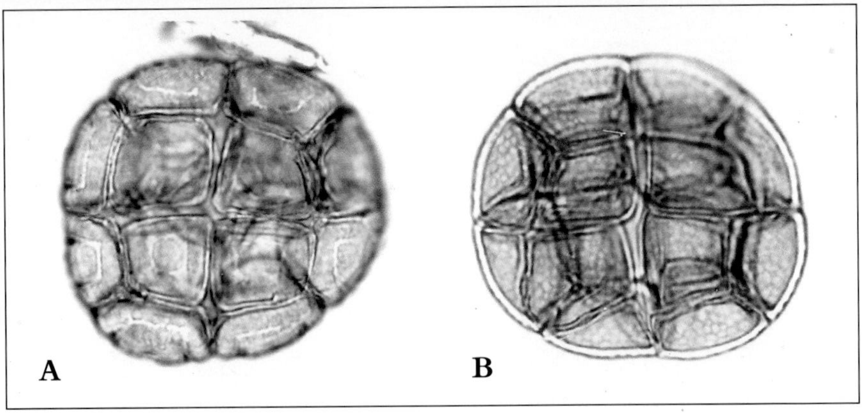

Plate 21 The original black and white light microscope photographs of reference pollen of Gympie *Acacia* collected from the herbarium. **A.** *Acacia aulacocarpa* has small, almost circular tectal 'islands' on the surface of the monads—compare with grain from tape-lift in plate 20C; **B**. *Acacia cowleana*, with a dimpled surface and no tectal islands on the monad surfaces—similar to, but larger than, the grain on a tape-lift in plate 22D. Magnification x 850.

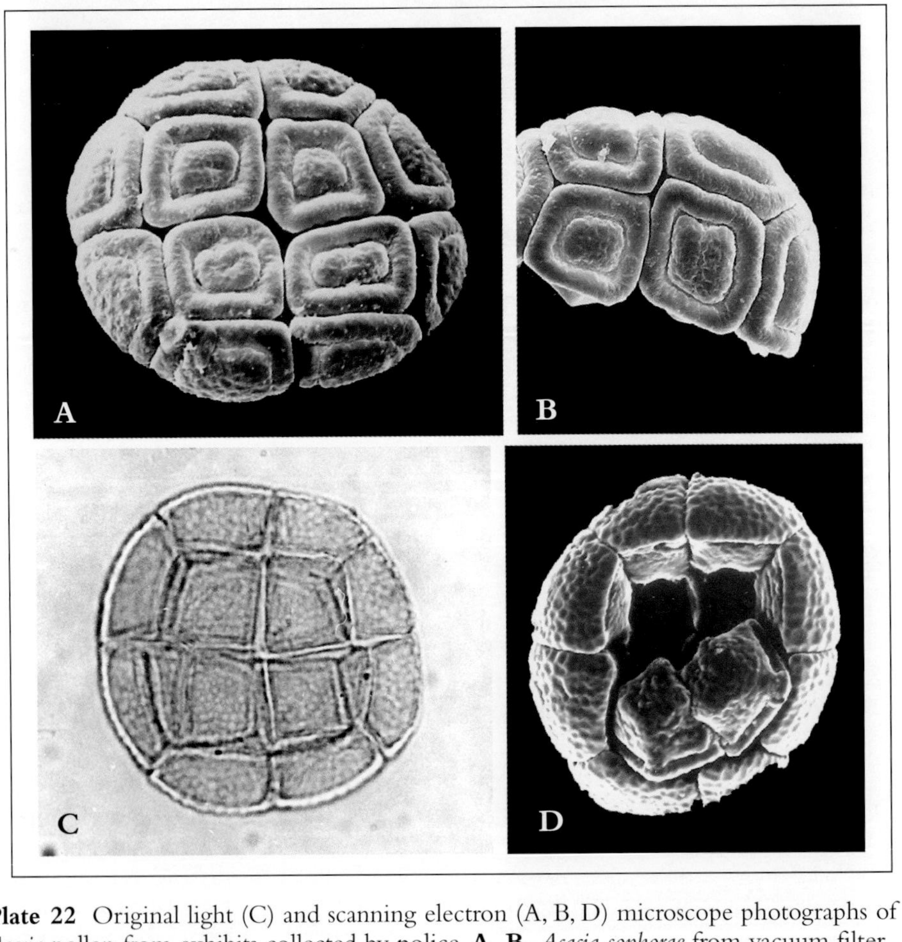

Plate 22 Original light (C) and scanning electron (A, B, D) microscope photographs of *Acacia* pollen from exhibits collected by police. **A, B.** *Acacia sophorae* from vacuum filter sample from victim's car; **C.** Dimpled *Acacia* grain from vacuum filter sample from victim's car; **D.** Dimpled *Acacia* grain on processed tape-lift from suspect's jeans. Magnification x 1200.

Wattles and their Pollen

Most people, if asked to nominate the most dominant plant genus in the Australian landscape, would propose the genus *Eucalyptus*. But they would be wrong. The true king (or queen) of the Australian landscape is *Acacia*, or wattle as it is commonly known. More than 950 wattle species are currently recognised in Australia,[3] whereas *Eucalyptus* contained only about 650 species before its recent division into several genera.[4] Ask the same people what is Australia's national flower emblem, or what do the Australian green and gold sporting colours represent, and they would get it right—wattle. Wattles do occur elsewhere in the world—but Australia has most of them.

There are about 1200 wattle species worldwide and the only continents where this genus doesn't occur naturally are Europe and Antarctica. It occurs in all climatic regions in Australia and, although the greatest species diversity is in the south-west of Western Australia and along the Great Dividing Range in eastern Australia, wattle plants are also a prominent feature of the desert landscapes. Aside from its wonderful display of yellow flowers, wattle is a versatile economic resource in the form of wood products, fuel and tannin. Its seeds, resin, bark and wood were traditionally used by Aborigines for food, fuel, weapons, medicine and in rituals. Perhaps the midst of a stand of flowering wattles was a fitting place of rest for a young woman whose family had so embraced Australia as its own.

During my research on wattles I came across a website[5] that detailed the official proclamation of the Golden Wattle (*Acacia pycnantha*) as Australia's national floral emblem by Sir Ninian Stephen on 1 September 1988. The first day of September is officially Wattle Day. It wasn't this that caught my eye, but a verse from a Spicer's desk diary on the page for 1 September that was quoted:

The soft golden wattle blooms brightly in Spring;
So why do we still call the daffodil, king?

I don't collect verses, but I wrote this one down because I didn't know what it meant and hoped it would come to me later.

Daffodils were again brought to my attention several weeks later as I sat listening to the voice of a clairvoyant on an audio tape sent to me by Samantha Hall's family. It is quite common for families, and even police, to ask for the help of a clairvoyant in a homicide case. Although the 'findings' of a clairvoyant can't be used as evidence in court, police may use them to help further their investigation; and for families, it helps the grieving process whether they are sceptics or not.

The morning after Samantha Hall's body was found and identified, but before her death was widely publicised, her elder brother was asked by his parents to contact a well-known clairvoyant to find out if she could help them learn what had actually happened to Sam. Although a confirmed sceptic, Sam's brother agreed to do this and went to see the clairvoyant that afternoon. He gave a piece of Sam's jewellery to the clairvoyant, and told her only that it was his sister's and that she'd been murdered. She held it in her hand to gain a sense of the person it belonged to, and proceeded to tell him what she knew of this person. Sam's brother taped the reading.

The clairvoyant began with the feeling of lying under bushes and a man leaning down over her picking something up. He was an outdoor type of man, a short sleeves man, a man with strong arms and hands. Then she shifted to another view—there was a woman offering daffodils. This was all in the first five minutes of the session. Later she revealed that Sam had been murdered in her own home, as Lyn and Malcolm had suspected.

The information the clairvoyant provided about the circumstances surrounding Sam's death that day, and on one other occasion, was chillingly accurate. For example, she described in minute detail that only a person who had seen her body would know, the injuries to Sam's body and what she was wearing at the time she was killed. She also described how Sam was killed and how her body was moved to the place under bushes. Throughout this first session with Sam's brother, and during a second session with Lyn and Malcolm Hall, flowers came into the clairvoyant's view again several times. 'Spring flowers...where there were a lot of flowers...are they daffodils?' was one such comment. No one told her that there were flowers at the crime scene.

It was another month before I realised what the small verse in the Spicer's desk diary was alluding to. The solution to many problems that seem to go round in circles unsolved, and many of my most brilliant, brilliant ideas, come into my head while I'm having a shower. I give credit for these ideas to my 'shower fairy'. It seems I have a new fairy—the 'watering fairy'—for it was while watering my sad roses that it came to me. Consider this:

Scene: A classroom of seven-year-old Australians.

'Class, who can name a yellow flower?' the teacher asks.

'Miss, me miss', echoes through the room as eager arms wave in the air to be chosen.

'Yes Johnny?'

'A daffodil, Miss.'

'Yes, that's right, Johnny. Good boy.'

How many of us think of wattles as having flowers? Individual wattle flowers are quite small—but they are massed together to form an inflorescence that is either an elongated 'spike' or a dense fluffy spherical head (Plates 12 and 13). 'Real' flowers are roses, daffodils and daisies, flowers that we cut and gather in bunches and put in vases, aren't they? Well, so our predominantly European heritage has taught us to believe.

Although her comments about flowers and daffodils were of little significance to Sam's family at the time they visited the clairvoyant, and the wattle–daffodil verse meant little to me at first, it finally dawned on me that it was yellow flowers that had helped to find Samantha Hall's murderer. Like Johnny, the clairvoyant had associated yellow flowers with daffodils, not wattles. And the Spicer's diary gently rebukes by asking Australians why, when we have so many native wattles, we associate yellow flowers with a flower not native to our country. Thank you 'watering fairy'.

When the police realised that the wattle flowers found in and on Samantha Hall's car might be significant to their investigation, they contacted a recently graduated botany major, Byron Steel. Steel was working on a doctoral thesis funded by a police grant and was an obvious choice. His thesis was to examine the variation in pollen assemblages produced by different vegetation types in Queensland, with emphasis on their possible use in forensic science. In the process of applying for the grant, Steel had given a presentation on the use of palynology in forensic science to officers from Scientific Section at Police Headquarters, Brisbane.

Although he had little experience in pollen morphology and pollen preparation, and no experience in criminal cases, Steel agreed to work on the case. One month after the discovery of Sam's body the police gave Steel the wattle flower found inside her car and a variety of exhibit samples (from Sam's car and clothing and the suspect's clothing) they hoped might contain wattle pollen. The police also gave Steel samples of wattle plant material collected from the crime scene at Noosa.

Steel's task was to determine if wattle pollen was present on the suspect's clothing and, if it was, to establish whether it was from the same species as the flower found in the victim's car. A positive result could associate the suspect with the victim's car—the car that police suspected was used to transport her body to the crime scene in Noosa where wattles had been blooming. But could the flower and any pollen found on the suspect's clothing have come from wattles growing in Gympie?

A week later the two arresting officers took Steel to Gympie to look for wattle plants along the path the suspect alleged he had taken on the evening of Friday 30 August 1996, and in other areas the suspect and victim frequented.

At first glance, Steel believed that the wattles growing in Gympie near the areas of interest were different from those police had collected samples from at the Noosa crime scene. To confirm this, he collected samples (30–40 cm sections) from the Gympie wattles and took them, and the wattle samples police had collected from Noosa, to the Brisbane Herbarium to have a botanist officially identify the species they came from.

Steel was right. The herbarium botanist identified the plant samples and confirmed that the wattle species at the Noosa crime scene were different from those that grew in Gympie near the areas of interest. This was excellent news. All Steel had to do now was to compare the pollen of these different species with pollen from the flower found in the deceased's car and with any wattle pollen grains he might find on the exhibits police had given him. This would determine if Samantha Hall's body had been transported to Noosa in her own car, and possibly provide police with enough evidence to arrest a suspect.

It was not to be so simple. All the wattle pollen looked the same to Steel—and he was unsure how to prepare the pollen samples collected from the exhibits. His inexperience in pollen morphology and preparation had caught up with him. By the time he came to the decision that he couldn't provide police with the information they wanted, it was six months after the investigation had begun and the investigating team still had no evidence with which to arrest a suspect. Steel suggested to the police that electron microscopy be used. He couldn't do it but he knew just the person—a fellow student, somewhat longer in the tooth than himself and who spent much of her time communing with electron microscopes and pollen. My career in forensic palynology was about to be launched.

Wattle pollen is unusual in that what we call a wattle pollen grain is not actually a single pollen grain. It is a number of pollen grains, usually 12 or 16, and sometimes 10, that are fused together to form a composite circular grain. The individual grains are called monads, and the composite grain is called a polyad (Plate 14).

Wattles are insect pollinated and, as a rule of thumb, pollen from each species should be morphologically different. The chances that I could distinguish between the pollen from those wattle species that grew in Noosa and the pollen from wattle species that grew in Gympie were quite good.

Although I had never worked in any detail with wattle pollen, I had come across a fossil grain in 1981, while working on my Honours thesis. This grain came from a low-grade coal some 40 metres below the surface of the ground on the western edge of the Nullarbor Plain. In the early 1980s exploration for oil shale as a future oil resource was being conducted by a number of Western Australian mining companies. To find the oil shale and determine how large the deposit was, boreholes were drilled in areas that were thought to have been near the ancient coastlines created by the sea level rises during the Eocene (approximately 58–37 million years ago) and Miocene (approximately 24–5 million years ago).

Oil shale and coal are the products of plant material being buried rapidly in swampy areas. This rapid burial prevents oxygen-loving bacteria from attacking and decaying the plant material. As more plant material is deposited on top, the plant material below is compressed. Depending on the depth below the surface of the ground and the type of plant material deposited, the compressed vegetation will form into peat, oil shale or coal.

The Eocene encompasses some 21 million years of the Earth's history and is divided into Early, Middle and Late Eocene. My Honours thesis project was to describe the ancient pollen species from some of the Eocene sedimentary rocks that two boreholes cut through, and try to work out in which part of the Eocene the sediments were deposited. This I would do by comparing the pollen assemblages they contained with Eocene pollen assemblages from south-eastern Australia that had already been dated.

In 1981 it was thought that during the Eocene, southern Australia, from the west to the east, supported the same type of vegetation. The pollen that I found in the ancient sediments from the western margin of the Nullarbor Plain did not wholly support this theory and led me to believe that the vegetation in Western Australia at that time was different from that of eastern Australia. There were more pollen grains from ancient members of the Proteaceae, the plant family that includes grevilleas and banksias. And then there were wattles.

The discovery of a wattle pollen grain in my samples was met with some scepticism from my more learned eastern Australian colleagues. Such an ancient fossil pollen grain of wattle had not been found in Australia before. Did wattle really grow 40 million years ago along the edge of the Nullarbor Plain in Western Australia? Or was it a stray grain from a modern plant that had found its way into my sample in the laboratory? More recent discoveries of similarly old wattle pollen elsewhere in Australia have gone some way to vindicating my discovery, but a cloud still hangs over it. The microscope slide in which the grain was found has dried out and the grain can no longer be found. It seems that wattle pollen and I have an affinity, and perhaps unfinished business.

Sex Without Legs

My entry into the field of forensic science was accidental, and surprising. I was in the right place at the right time and with the right academic and technical qualifications. In retrospect, I shouldn't have been so surprised that my skills in palynology might lead to forensic work. All palynologists are detectives. Every use of pollen analysis—and there are many—involves using pollen as a clue to solve a mystery or problem.

What I still find surprising is that after beginning my working life as a Physical Education teacher I'm now working in forensic science. Most of my generation's parents and grandparents began their working lives in a trade or profession that they remained in for the rest of their working lives, receiving the obligatory gold watch on their retirement. A considerable number of my generation have done the same. But not so for our progeny. Technology, and perhaps the current trend of short-term contracts rather than lifetime employment, has allowed many of them to cross traditional career borders and have several 'careers' in their working lifetime. I'm in the minority in my generation and need a few fingers to count my career changes. None of these changes was planned—they just happened, and each change of direction stemmed from an interest that was tangential to my last occupation.

Such occupation tangents were also common in the scientific world of the seventeenth and eighteenth centuries. The scientists who first reported that pollen from different species looked different, and described their morphology, were predominantly medical practitioners or physiologists. Some later moved on to other fields of science such as chemistry. Like me, they discovered interests and passions they had not contemplated before and followed where they led. It was an exciting time in the history of science. A new tool, the compound microscope, revolutionised the scientific study of animals and plants by opening up the fascinating world of microscopic anatomy.

Although simple magnifying glasses have probably been around since the ancient Greeks, they are not strong enough to study pollen. The lens in a magnifying glass is a bi-convex piece of glass that bends light rays, and where the bent rays join and diverge they form an enlarged image of the object being viewed through the lens. The best common magnifying glasses today can only magnify objects 10 to 20 times their actual size—conventionally written as x 10 or x 20. When two or more lenses are used, the amount they magnify a specimen is the product of the strength of each lens. For example, if two x 10 lenses are used they will magnify a specimen x 100. If a x 10 and a x 100 lens are used, the image they produce will be x 1000 the actual size of a specimen.

The compound microscope, developed in 1665 by the English experimental scientist Hooke, was a simple brass tube with three lenses—one at each end and another in the middle. Almost 40 years later, a microscope with a screw focus was developed so specimens could remain in one position while the tube containing the lenses could be moved up and down to focus on different parts of a three-dimensional object.

Throughout history each new advance in the capability of microscopes has produced a corresponding advance in the knowledge and application of palynology. Without microscopes we would still consider pollen to be flowers' dust and believe that plants don't reproduce sexually—and there would be no palynology.

Perhaps the greatest mystery that the study of pollen has solved is its function in the plant world. There's evidence that the ancient Assyrians knew pollen was a useful part of plants but didn't associate it with sexual reproduction. They knew that if the yellow dust produced by some date palms was shaken over the flowers of other date palms, the date crop from the dusted palms would be greater than that of the flowering palms that had not been dusted. We know today that date palms are insect pollinated and unisexual—they are either male or female.

The dusting of palms is depicted in stone murals dating back as far as 860 BC.[2] In the fifth century BC Herodotus, the first Greek historian, reported that date palms were either male or female. This explanation for the increase in date crops after dusting was not accepted. A century later, Aristotle, the great Greek philosopher and scientist, denied the existence of sexual differentiation in plants because they were non-motile—in other words, they had no legs.

Aristotle and his teacher Plato were two of the most exceptional thinkers who lived. Their philosophies, although often opposing, underlie much of

Western philosophy today. Whereas Plato's method of searching for the truth was based on assumption and deduction, Aristotle's approach to knowledge was that of an experimental scientist. He collected evidence by observation and experimentation and drew careful conclusions supported by the evidence. He believed that all theory must follow demonstrable fact. These are the principles on which modern scientific research is based today.

How could the father of the modern scientific method get it so wrong? Quite easy. Although one of Aristotle's passions was the structure of living things and he analysed the parts of organisms in terms of their purpose, he didn't have a tool with which to examine their finer details—and, of course, plants don't have legs.

Despite Aristotle's denial of sex in plants, the fact that pollen played a sexual role in plant reproduction must have become common knowledge by the time of Pliny, 350 years later, who called pollen the material of fertilisation. It would be 16 centuries before humans developed the compound microscope and used scientific methodology to study the form and function of pollen and confirm Pliny's observation. Aristotle's scientific method persisted in the Arab world but was forgotten in Europe. Arab scholars re-introduced it to Europe in the thirteenth century, laying the foundations for a resurgence of scientific enquiry.

In the European scientific community of the seventeenth century, theories about nature required rigorous study and conclusive evidence in the Aristotelian tradition if they were to be accepted by fellow scientists—just as they do today. My work, like that of all modern-day scientists, is based on this precept, but I still have a fondness for the days of Pliny, when observations about nature were based on the fruits of its annual cycles and agricultural practices were based on this common knowledge. No matter the reason for it, if it works, keep doing it. In the modern era much time and money has been spent on scientific research to prove beyond doubt what is often common knowledge derived from experiences like those of the Assyrians.

The first scientists to look at pollen in any detail did so out of sheer curiosity. It was another small part of nature to look at with the newly developed compound microscope. At that time, in the mid-seventeenth century, European scientists still didn't know what function pollen served in the plant world and there was much speculation as to whether it was a useful part of plants or an incidental secretion. Many botanists at that time compared plant organs and their function with the organs of animals. One scientist even suggested that the role of pollen was similar to that of the menstrual flow in female mammals. Another, on observing insects visiting flowers, suggested that pollen was produced to provide food for insects—it was an example of nature's generosity. Although some scientists speculated that pollen had something to do with plant sexuality, they were shouted down by their peers.

In the two decades that followed the development of the compound microscope, the study of microscopic plant anatomy boomed. The founders of this new discipline, the Englishman Nehemiah Grew and the Italian Marcello Malpighi, separately published works that included descriptions and illustrations of pollen grains. They called them 'Particles' or 'Globulets' respectively. In his *Anatomy of Plants*, published in 1682, Grew reported that these Particles '...are of different size and form in different species, but those of the same species are alike'.[2] This simple fact forms the basis of palynology today. There was no special terminology with which to describe what he saw down the microscope, so Grew compared the different shapes of pollen with objects that can be seen with the naked eye, such as seeds and fruit, and even a Dutch cheese. It's possible that Grew knew of the fertilising function of pollen, but the existence of plant sexuality is credited to Rudolph Camerarius, a German who in 1694 provided abundant evidence of the role of anthers and pollen in the sexual reproduction of plants from his study of mulberry trees.

For Grew and Malpighi the study of pollen was not a lifetime occupation. Both men were physicians with interests in the comparison of animal and plant morphology and pollen was only a small part of their research. There was no further development of the microscope in the 150 years that followed, and the study of microscopic plant parts stagnated until the early nineteenth century.

By 1824 the most modern microscope was capable of magnifying objects x 500. The botanical artist Francis Bauer, who worked in England with the legendary botanist Robert Brown under the patronage of Sir Joseph Banks, sparked the next surge of interest in pollen morphology. His pencil sketches of pollen from 175 species are now held in the British Museum. Some of the grains he drew were pollen of wattle species. Bauer and Brown apparently recognised the importance of pollen characteristics in the description of plant species, and in many of Bauer's paintings of plants he illustrated their pollen. Sadly this is not done today.

From the 1830s to the 1850s there was a great increase in the knowledge of pollen morphology. At the same time, aspects other than pollen's physical appearance were investigated. These included the function of pores, grains' ability to expand and contract in water, their arrangement in anthers, the pollen tubes they grew and the structure, surface sculpture and chemistry of their walls. This was pure scientific research—the search for knowledge for the sake of knowledge itself. Oh, for the days when artists and scientists had patrons who supported their work, or had jobs for life to pursue their passion.

Pure research, or blue-sky research as it is sometimes called, has provided the modern world with many of its most important discoveries. Unfortunately, those who provide funding for research today often overlook this fact. Scientific research is now predominantly driven by the projected commercial application of its findings. It's unlikely that early researchers of pollen envisaged that their studies would eventually have economic uses, but their research has paid its dues and pollen analysis now has many commercial applications.

A Versatile Investigative Tool

Although the forensic use of pollen and spores didn't begin until the early 1960s, other economic and scientific uses for their study evolved during the first half of the twentieth century. As these commercial applications grew, a name was sought for this new discipline and its applications. The word palynology was proposed in the 1940s[6] to cover both the academic study of pollen and spores and the commercial and scientific applications of pollen analysis. Pollen means dust in Latin, and the word palynology was derived from the Greek verb *palunein*, which means to sprinkle or dust.[7]

The scope of palynology has since broadened and now includes the study of other plant and some animal microfossils that are acid-resistant. Because they're acid-resistant, it's possible to extract them from sediments, soil and dust by using acids to get rid of most of the minerals. Collectively, all microscopic particles studied by palynologists are called palynomorphs. They include fungal spores, cysts from marine and freshwater algae, remains of extinct microscopic organisms and fragments of plant and animal tissues. They're all found in sedimentary rocks and have chemical compositions that resist degradation if they are deposited in favourable conditions.

There are two major divisions within palynology. In broad terms, Quaternary palynology, the study of palynomorphs from the last 2 million years, is a tool for geographers, archaeologists, botanists and geologists. Palaeopalynology, the study of older palynomorphs, is the domain of geologists and palaeobotanists. Today there are many specialist areas within each division.

Quaternary palynology and palaeopalynology use different methods of preparation and analysis. Traditionally there has been a wide gap between the two, and it's not uncommon to hear palaeopalynologists refer to themselves as 'real' palynologists. Being one of them myself, I'm guilty as charged. Having recently worked alongside Quaternary palynologists, however, I now recognise that both disciplines have their virtues and I use methods from both in my forensic work.

Pollen was first used as an investigative tool in 1916, when E. J. Lennart von Post, a Norwegian geologist, presented his research on pollen analysis of Quaternary peat bogs. Tens of metres of peat can build up over time in shallow lakes, swamps and marshes where plants grow rapidly and are equally speedily buried by their successors. The fossil plant material in each layer of peat is a record of plants that grew in the area when the peat formed. During the Quaternary era the Earth experienced quite rapid changes in climate. Rapid, that is, in terms of geological time, which means these changes occurred over thousands, rather than millions, of years. During the coldest periods, ice-sheets covered Canada, the northern USA, Europe, New Zealand, Tasmania and south-eastern Australia. These glacial periods were followed by warmer periods called interglacials. As the climate changed, so did the vegetation.

In the early 1900s European scientists looking for evidence of these past climate changes searched in peat bogs for well-preserved fossil leaves, wood and seeds. Von Post's research showed that pollen was more plentiful than large well-preserved plant material in peat bogs, and that sequential vegetation and climatic changes could easily be recognised by studying pollen at different levels in the peat.

Prior to von Post's 1916 work, the study of pollen had been the domain of botanists. Gradually over the next twenty years pollen analysis began to be used by other disciplines to study sediments in lakes, swamps, peat bogs, caves and alluvial deposits. Geographers began to use it to measure climate change. Palaeobotanists and geologists studied it to understand the evolution of plants. And archaeologists used pollen to investigate the beginnings of agriculture.

The next advance in pollen analysis evolved in the mid-1930s, with the use of fossil pollen and spores to link, or match up, sedimentary rock layers (strata) of the same age, but occurring in different localities. This is called stratigraphic correlation. Although the techniques developed to correlate sedimentary rocks are used in coalfields and other areas of mining, the greatest economic use of palynology in the last 50 years has been in the petroleum industry—in the search for oil and gas. These natural resources that keep our modern society in the manner to which it is accustomed are products of the anaerobic (oxygen-free) decay of plant material contained in marine and terrestrial sedimentary rocks. The marine contribution comes from microscopic algae that is part of plankton.

Sedimentation means the settling out of particles in suspension or the deposition of particles in a layer. Sedimentary particles are solid materials physically deposited by wind, water or ice (glaciers), or dissolved substances chemically precipitated from water bodies.[8] Physically deposited sediments are derived from the erosion of pre-existing rocks and the remains of animals and plants. Pollen is a sedimentary particle. As each new layer of sediment is deposited in environments such as rivers and their floodplains, lakes, deltas, meteorite craters and continental shelves, it buries the previous layer. Therefore, any one layer of sediment is older than the one above it. As more layers of sediment accumulate on top, the sediments below are compressed to form rock.

The organic remains encapsulated in each successive sedimentary layer provide a historical record of plants and animals that existed in the environment when the sediment was deposited. It follows that fossil-bearing sediments deposited in different places at the same time in the Earth's history will usually contain some similar plant and animal fossils. Natural evolutionary processes and those prompted by climatic change and catastrophic events, such as the meteorite impact that wiped out the dinosaurs, produce marked differences in the assemblages of animal and plant remains in each major rock layer. From these similarities and differences it's possible to identify discrete layers of fossil assemblages based on the presence or absence, or abundance or paucity of certain fossil types, in particular palynomorphs. It is these fossil layers, or zones, that are used in oil exploration to help correlate sedimentary rock strata (layers) in different areas. From this a cross-section map of what the rocks look like beneath the Earth's surface can be drawn to help explorationists decide where, and how far, to drill for the oil-bearing rocks.

Correlating rock strata is not as simple as it seems. Each major period of deposition may occur over a period of thousands, or even millions, of years, and great depths of sedimentary rock are built up. Many oil wells today are drilled not through metres but through kilometres of sedimentary rock. These rocks are rarely as flat as they were when they were laid down. The Earth's tectonic processes (the movement of the crustal plates) cause folding and faulting that bends, uplifts or lowers sections of sedimentary rocks. This provides a jigsaw puzzle for those searching for oil and gas. For example, a particular layer of sediment may be 700 metres below the surface in one place, but only 300 metres below the surface in another nearby, or it may have petered out altogether because it has been eroded at the Earth's surface (see diagrams page 79).

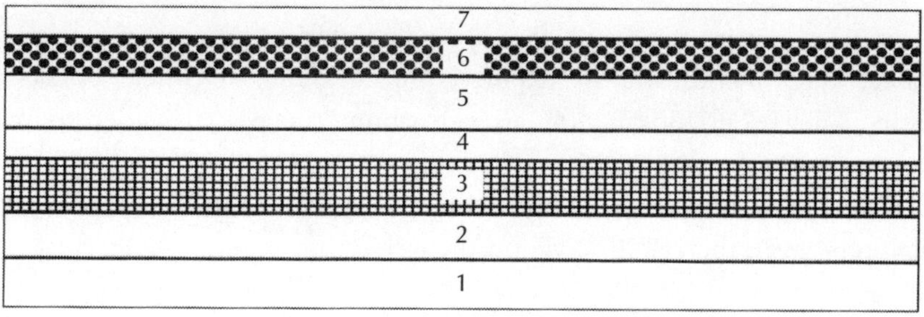

Horizontal sedimentary rock layers before folding and faulting.

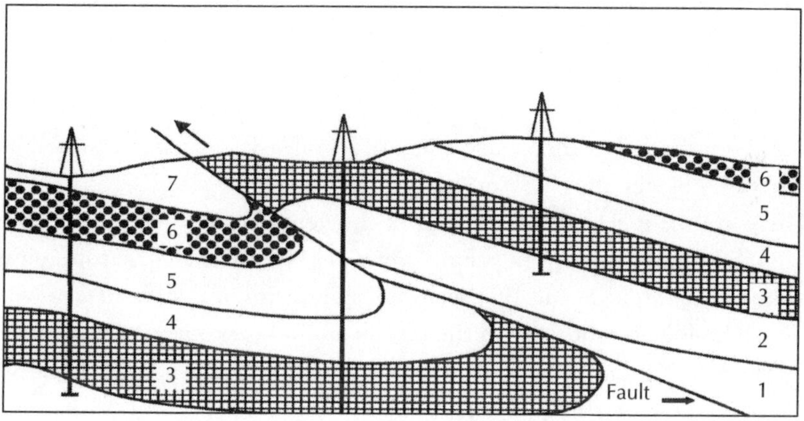

Sedimentary rock layers after they have been folded and faulted, *showing different depths to which oil wells may have to be drilled to reach the same layer.*

What does ancient sedimentation have to do with forensic palynology? Lots. Soil is a sediment and, although the majority of palynomorphs in it are from the contemporary environment, soil may also contain palynomorphs from ancient sedimentary rocks that have been exposed to weathering. These 'reworked' sedimentary particles, together with pollen and spores from the vegetation that exists today, can provide a very distinctive pollen assemblage with which to link a suspect to a crime scene.

Palynomorphs in sediments, soil and accumulated dust all tell a story, whether they are several millions of years old or a couple of days old. They're clues to past environments and events. Sediment and soil form the base layer of our environment and dust covers almost everything in it, so it's not surprising that many scientific disciplines use palynology as an investigative tool.

Besides geology, botany, archaeology and geography, palynology is used in immunology, zoology, entomology and a host of environmental sciences. It's also used by government and private bodies such as customs, fisheries and wildlife, water boards, import–export companies and, of course, police and lawyers. They're all looking for answers about the past in order to make decisions about the future.

Do we arrest this person for breaking and entering? Yes. They have a rare pollen type from the crime scene on their clothing.

Have we reached the oil reservoir yet? No. We'll keep drilling.

Will the new dam flood the feeding ground of an endangered species? Yes, we can tell from pollen in the faeces that the plants they eat will be flooded. We'll have to move this species population to another site or redirect the dam from that area.

What pollen causes my hay fever? Grasses. I'll get rid of the offending grass from my garden.

Did Neanderthal people bury their dead on a bed of flowers? Yes. They weren't such brutes after all. And the list goes on.

There are many people in sections of the general and scientific communities and in industry for whom palynology would be an invaluable tool—if only they knew about it. Some of the responsibility for this lack of knowledge about palynology might lie with the petroleum industry. Fierce competition in the early years of the industry meant that much in-house palynological work was kept secret. Companies also paid their palynologists well, and what person in their right mind would deny themselves a well-paid job in the petroleum industry to find out who murdered who or what certain animals eat and be paid a measly sum for it? Not many. Aside from economic reasons, forensic palynology doesn't appeal to many palynologists because it requires court appearances and may attract litigation.

For those who do take the risk of promoting and carrying out alternative uses of palynology, the financial rewards are not great, but the work is interesting and challenging. Instead of sitting in air-conditioned offices doing routine microscopy and analysis, they can be found in the Gobi Desert in Mongolia collecting sediments from a dinosaur dig, or visiting crime scenes and providing expert evidence in court.

My first inkling that palynology could be lucrative came towards the end of a boom in the petroleum industry. It was 1980. I'd finished my three-year degree in geology and was looking for an Honours project. One lecturer was keen for me to work on palynology, but I was more interested in sedimentology and micropalaeontology. He finally convinced me that the toils of systematic palynology, the painstaking description of fossil pollen, would be worth it the day he leaned over his desk and quietly said, 'You can make a lot of money from palynology'. And I did…for the first four years after my graduation. As a consultant palynologist to the petroleum and mining industries I was able to work at home on my own microscope, have babies and earn more than most women in full-time jobs.

This ideal situation didn't last. The oil price plunged and the industry cut back on non-essential services, including palynology. Palynologists who were fully employed by petroleum companies were stood down or moved into mainstream geology. Others began new careers or worked as consultants. The flush of new palynology consultants in the market place impacted on the established consulting groups. For four years I'd been part of a consulting group comprising two men and two women. Equality of the sexes. Because fewer contracts were now available the men took over most of the work. They had families to support. I lost all of my customers except one. A company in which the majority of geologists were women! This male dominance of palynological consulting to the Australian petroleum industry persists today.

At first, with small children to keep me busy, I wasn't bothered by the lack of work, but eventually my passion for all things pollen got the better of me. I conducted private research and published a paper on it. Shortly thereafter a mining company approached me with an offer of a PhD project and a little funding. I accepted.

My PhD project was initially based on palynostratigraphy—the study of palynomorph assemblages in ancient sediments and, based on the type of palynomorphs present, the division of these sediments into zones representing different periods of time and/or periods of deposition. This direction was short-lived. I discovered the joys of electron microscopy and the fascinating field of comparative fossil and modern pollen morphology. It could reveal the evolutionary history of today's plants and from this, the structure of vegetation communities that grew when the ancient sediments were deposited. I was off on a tangent and my PhD supervisors berated me to get back on track. I didn't, and on graduating, instead of being more qualified for a job in the petroleum and mining industries, I found myself heading for academia.

My experience with modern pollen has led me into other applications of palynology beside its forensic use. I've examined cow dung, kangaroo and emu poo and scat (faeces) of the Yellow-bellied Glider for environmental studies. I've looked at pollen collected by bees to determine what plants they visit. I've investigated pollen trapped by cannabis leaves to work out where the cannabis was grown, and I've captured and identified airborne pollen to aid asthma and allergy research. Along the way I became interested in the role plant microfossils (pollen and spores) play in unravelling the history of plants on Earth.

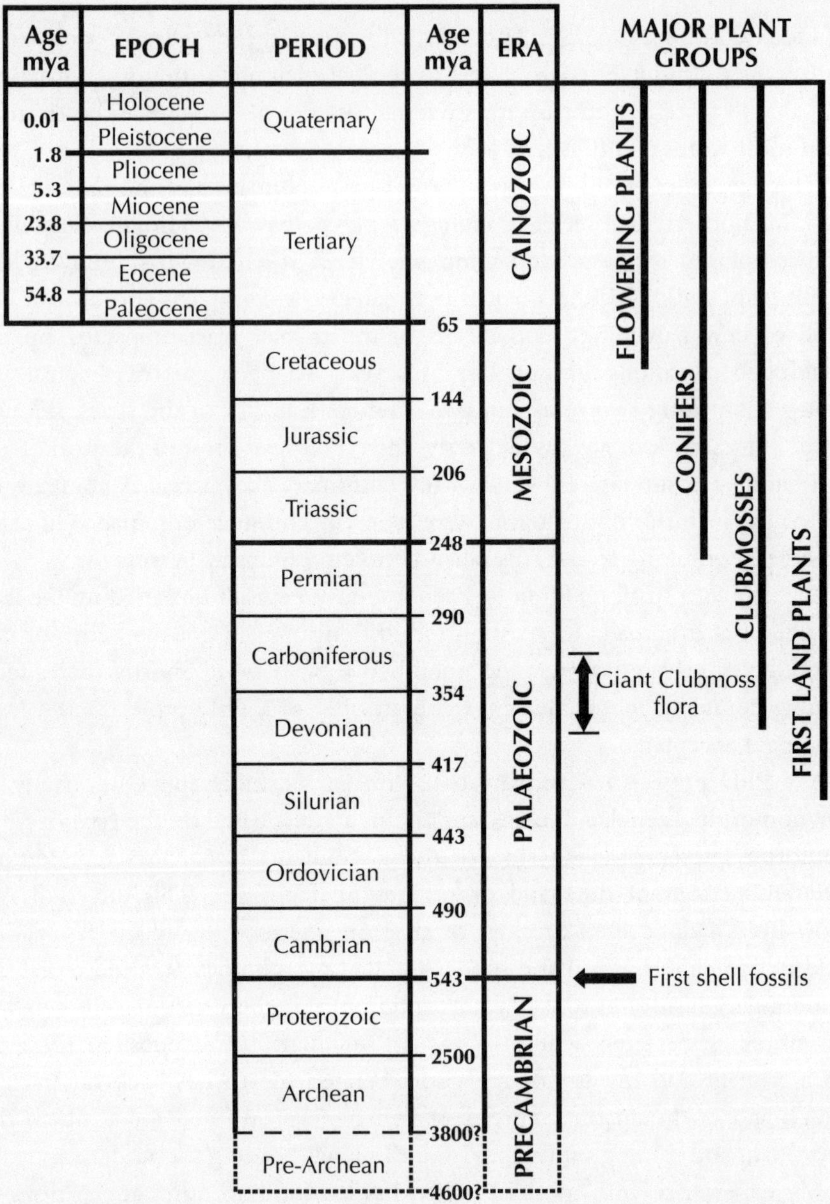

***Geological time scale**, showing the approximate time ferns, pines (conifers), clubmosses and flowering plants evolved.*

Plant macrofossils—such as wood, leaves, fruit, seeds and flowers—in sediments deposited in ancient swamps and areas where floods have buried them quickly, reveal what ancient plants looked like. Mary White's 1986 *The*

Greening of Gondwana describes the 400-million-year story of Australia's vegetation and illustrate spectacular macrofossils. The Giant Clubmoss flora that dominated the landscape between about 385 and 325 million years ago must have been stunning. It was a time when relatives of the small horsetails and clubmosses of today were giant trees. However, macrofossils are relatively rare and only represent plants that fossilised well and grew near waterlogged areas. On the other hand, microfossils—pollen, spores and small fragments of other dispersed plant material—are found in a wider variety of sediments and can reveal the spatial distribution of ancient plants and the existence of plants for which no macrofossils are known.

There is little evidence of flowering plants until about 120 million years ago in the mid-Cretaceous—before the dinosaurs died out. Children's story books illustrating dinosaurs with flowers are not fanciful after all. Flowering plants became relatively common by the early Cainozoic, and today dominate our vegetation. The Cainozoic, the period that covers the last 66 million years of the Earth's history, is often called 'The Age of Flowering Plants'. The geological time scale opposite shows approximately when the major plant groups appeared.

Petroleum palynologists study spores, pollen and marine algal cysts (single-celled aquatic organisms) called dinoflagellates. Earlier I spoke of the different ways in which palaeopalynologists and Quaternary palynologists prepare and analyse pollen. Petroleum palynologists are palaeopalynologists. Those who are experts in the study of spores and pollen are usually specialists in fossil spores of mosses, ferns and extinct plants and in the pollen of ancient relatives of today's pines, cycads and ginkgos (Gymnosperms). These were the plants that dominated the vegetation on Earth before the arrival of flowering plants. Petroleum palynologists are rarely interested in forensic palynology because few of them work with the more modern pollen and spores that are normally the province of forensic work. Palynologists who work in Quaternary and modern palynology, or in Cainozoic palaeopalynology, are the ones who are drawn into forensic work because of their familiarity with pollen from flowering plants. Note I say drawn into, not employed in. To my knowledge there's only one person fully employed as a forensic palynologist, although I suspect that's about to change. The rest of us spend half or slightly more of our time working as forensic scientists, but we're also funded by palynology projects in geology, geography, botany or archaeology.

Professor Vaughn M. Bryant Jr, Head of the Anthropology Department at Texas A&M University, is an example of a person being drawn into various kinds of palynology, including forensic. In an article titled 'Reader of the invisible dust'[9] he relates how he was employed to coordinate a palynology project while working on a Master's degree in anthropology. After accepting the job he went home and looked up the word palynologist! Vaughn's doctoral project was to be on Quaternary vegetational history, but he went off on a tangent, as we are wont to do, and became interested in the contents of human coprolites (fossil faecal remains). He became the first person to study all the different contents of coprolites, including seeds, bones, hair, feathers, parasites and, of course, pollen and other plant material.

As well as his archaeological research and the odd forensic case, Vaughn's palynological detective work includes melissopalynology, the palynology of honey. Why would anyone study honey? Honey is essentially pollen in syrup. Bees collect pollen and nectar. Mixed together they make honey. Honey collected from beehives will contain pollen from plants that were flowering in the area. Boutique honeys are marketed as coming from a particular plant, whereas generic supermarket honey is a mixture of honeys from different areas and plants. For quarantine and political reasons, many countries restrict the importation of honey. The mixing of cheap imported honey with more expensive local honey to increase the profit margin is illegal. But it's still done. From the pollen in honey a melissopalynologist can determine if it has been doctored, if it comes from particular plants as advertised or from the country it is alleged to be from.

Forensic pollen analysis of honey was conducted in New South Wales many years ago by a now retired colleague of mine. An elderly gent bought a loaf of bread that purportedly contained honey. On eating the bread he couldn't taste any honey and went back to the bakery to confront the baker. The baker insisted that the bread contained honey. Not convinced, the elderly gent sued the baker. My colleague examined the loaf of bread bought by the gentleman for pollen. No pollen was found. Another loaf advertised as containing honey was later bought from the same baker. It contained a lot of pollen, and therefore honey. The elderly gent won his case.

The examples of the use of pollen as an investigative tool that have been discussed here only touch the surface of the current use and future potential of palynology. When I agreed to work on the Samantha Hall homicide case I knew little about the use of palynology outside of its geological applications. I did know that palynology had been used to solve crimes, but I hadn't read about it. Like Vaughn Bryant, I had some homework to do.

Archaeological palynology is the most closely related type of palynology to forensic palynology. It can tell us what ancient people ate, the crops they grew and what they used pottery containers and woven baskets for, and shed light on their burial practices and rituals. In recent years nautical archaeologists have collected fossil pollen from shipwrecks to help determine what cargoes the ships carried, their port of origin and what artefacts were used for.

There is even evidence from the grave of a Neanderthal man that he was buried on a bed of twigs and flowers. In Shanidar Cave, Iraq, pollen from seven different ornamental flowers was found in clusters in a Neanderthal grave.[10] The clustering of the grains indicated that whole flowers had been placed in the grave, and the position of the soil samples the pollen was recovered from appear to suggest that flowers were laid below, on top of and beside the body. Palynological investigations such as this, and of the Iceman known as Oetzi, and of the Shroud of Turin, could be called archaeological or forensic.

The frozen body of Oetzi, a man who lived in northern Italy 5300 years ago, was found by tourists in mountains near the Italian and Austrian border in 1991. Archaeologists and forensic scientists have worked together on his body and possessions to build a picture of the life he led and the circumstances of his death. Oetzi's age was determined by the density of his bones, and analyses of his gut contents showed that his last meal, eaten about eight hours before he died, consisted of unleavened bread, an unidentified plant and meat.

Palynology has played a major role in suggesting Oetzi's movements in the hours before his death, and the time of year he died. It was initially thought that he died in autumn because pollen in the ice surrounding him was from autumn-flowering plants. It's now known that this ice had thawed several times, and that the autumn pollen in it was a secondary feature deposited after Oetzi's death. More recently, small numbers of hop hornbeam pollen found in Oetzi's large intestine have suggested that he died in spring. Hop hornbeam flowers between March and June, the northern hemisphere's spring. This plant isn't known to have been used as a herb so its pollen was probably eaten by accident—on food or in water that Oetzi ingested, or trapped in saliva when he inhaled.

Pollen also provided clues about Oetzi's movements prior to his death. Hop hornbeam plants would have been growing in warmer conditions in the valley some five to six hours' walk from the mountain site where Oetzi's body was found. He may have eaten his last meal in the valley.

Many theories about why Oetzi was on the mountain and where he came from have been put forward. The recent discovery by X-ray of a stone arrowhead lodged in his shoulder implies that he may have bled to death after fleeing attackers.

Oetzi the Iceman was a homicide victim. We don't know who killed him or why he was killed but from pollen evidence we do know the time of year he died and where he probably had his last meal. Investigation of gut contents has been used in a number of forensic cases to trace a victim's movements before their death. If Oetzi was a man of today, pollen evidence might have helped to find his killer.

Grains of Truth

In simple terms forensic palynology is the use of pollen and spores to help solve crimes. At least I knew that much when I agreed to work on the Noosa murder case. Now I can define it in more detail. Forensic palynology is the comparison of pollen samples from crime scenes, victims, suspects and objects 'of interest' to prove or disprove a relationship between them. Fingerprint analysis and DNA profiling aim to make the same connections. Again, this is a broad definition, and there is more to forensic palynology than that. Whereas fingerprinting uses trace evidence from the human body to identify a particular person, and DNA profiling can also identify a particular plant or animal, palynology uses trace evidence from plants to determine where a person has been or the origin or travel history of objects and organic material.

Palynology has been instrumental in many convictions, but its value also lies in providing corroborative evidence—evidence that supports other lines of evidence; and in suggesting other areas or people to investigate. I call the latter 'pointing police in the right direction'. The serial rape case I worked on in Perth was a good example of this. Similarly, palynology can determine if a body or item has been transported to a discovery scene. Was the person murdered at the scene where their body was discovered? Or did the murder take place elsewhere? Soil on clothing or other items will contain tell-tale pollen.

Aside from murders and rapes, there are numerous types of criminal and civil cases in which palynology has been used. It has foiled illegal importers by revealing what country goods and foodstuffs have come from. Fraud has been detected from pollen in the ink of signed documents, and a taxidermist's stuffing in a museum exhibit has disproved its claimed country of origin. Goods transported by ship have been replaced with rocks or bags of soil, and the pollen or marine palynomorphs they contained have shown where the substitution took place—the port of departure, a port en route or the port of disembarkment. It was a nasty shock for one importer to find blocks of limestone in place of his whisky. Then there are illicit drugs.

Cannabis, cocaine and heroin will contain pollen from the area in which the plants they are derived from were grown, processed, and later 'cut' and packaged. 'Cutting' drugs is the process of mixing pure drugs with other substances to increase their weight and bulk before sale on the open market. Edward Stanley, of the New York Police Department Crime Laboratory, reported a case where a shipment of cocaine was seized in New York City.[11] Samples were sent for pollen analysis to determine its country of origin. Three different groups of pollen were found in the cocaine: one from plants that grow in Bolivia and Colombia, another from a forest type that grows in parts of the northern USA and adjoining Canada, and the third from weeds commonly growing in vacant lots in New York City and Manhattan Island. It was concluded that the cocaine originated in South America, was 'cut' and packaged in northern North America, and probably 'cut' again in New York City.

Cannabis is especially interesting. Its leaves are covered in small spines that trap pollen from other plants growing in the area. From this trapped pollen it's possible to tell if separate cannabis seizures are from the same crop and to determine in what region or country the cannabis was grown. Despite the practice of weeding out male cannabis plants, their pollen is often found on the clothing of people who tend the crops and in buildings where cannabis has been grown hydroponically. The leaf spines on clothing and in soil and buildings also tell tales. In a recent case I worked on, a combination of cannabis spines and pollen helped destroy an alibi.

The two earliest recorded cases in which palynology was used as evidence in court illustrate how pollen analysis can indicate where a crime scene may be or at what time of year a crime was committed. Both occurred in 1959, one in Austria and one in Sweden. They were first reported in English by Erdtman in 1969 in his *Handbook of Palynology*.[12]

In the Austrian case, a man disappeared near Vienna while on a trip down the Danube River. An intensive search for the man proved fruitless and police feared he had been murdered. On questioning a suspect and searching his room, police found a pair of boots with mud on their soles.

A geologist with the Austrian Geological Survey, Dr Wilhelm Klaus, examined the mud to determine where it might have come from. He found large amounts of alder and pine pollen, and a single fossil pollen grain that occurs in rock strata many millions of years old—a unique combination. From geological and vegetation maps of the area around Vienna he was able to pinpoint a very much smaller area where alder and pine grew together on rocks of the age in which the fossil pollen occurred. When confronted with this evidence, the suspect confessed and took police to the murder and burial site.

In the Swedish case, a woman went missing in May and her body was found one month later. But was she murdered at the discovery scene or somewhere else? The prosecution hired a pollen analyst to examine dirt on the woman's clothing and shoes. The defence did the same. Palynologists on both sides agreed that dirt on the woman's clothing and shoes was not from the site her body was found, but they drew quite different conclusions. The prosecution claimed the murder had taken place at another locality and that the body was transported to the discovery site. The defence claimed that the murder had taken place only a short distance from where the body was found.

The defence palynologist examined soil samples from other areas near where the body was found. He took into account what plants flowered in May and June, and therefore how the pollen spectra in the soil would be compositionally different in each of these months. In May there would be little grass pollen, whereas in June grass pollen would be common. In addition, the pollen assemblages from the crime scene and the clothing and shoes both contained the same indicator pollen—pollen that is rare and specific to certain environments. In this case, the environment in which the body was found. Also on the clothing and shoes was a rare combination of degraded clover pollen and well-preserved fungal spores. This same combination occurred in soil not far from the body. There are no reports on what view prevailed at the trial, but if I were judge or jury, I'd support the defence's argument.

A recent example of pollen assemblages from soil indicating that bodies have been moved is from the mass graves in Srebrenica, a Bosnian silver-mining town. It's estimated that during the Bosnia–Herzegovina war the Bosnian–Serb army executed some 8000 Muslims. The largest single massacre occurred over five days in July 1995, when about 2000 Muslim men and boys from Srebrenica were executed at a local football field and gymnasium. At these sites the bodies were placed in mass graves.

In an attempt to conceal the scale of the killings, the Bosnian–Serb forces later exhumed the primary mass graves and removed the bodies to smaller secondary graves scattered around the countryside. The bodies were exhumed hastily at night, and with them to the secondary grave sites went soil and rocks from the primary graves. After the war, forensic teams analysed soil and rocks associated with the human remains and artefacts with them. From the results they were able to determine where the people in the secondary graves had been executed and placed in the primary graves. Similar work has been done on the Kosovo mass graves.

There are two ways of comparing pollen samples. One compares the relative composition of pollen assemblages and the other concentrates on the identification of rare pollen types specific to a particular locality. It's ideal if both can be used. The majority of pollen in soil will be from wind-pollinated plants. This provides an overview of the vegetation in the immediate area and its surrounds, and is useful where two different vegetation types are involved. It's not difficult to tell the difference between a pollen assemblage from soil in a pine forest and one from a garden, vacant block, or eucalypt woodland. Pollen from animal- and insect-pollinated plants is rare by comparison in most dispersed pollen assemblages, but it can provide more specific evidence about the locality it came from.

Pollen from an insect-pollinated plant was used in a sexual assault case in New Zealand in 1996.[13] A woman raped in a driveway near ornamental shrubs recognised her assailant and reported the assault to police. The suspect denied having been where the rape occurred. During the struggle both the victim and assailant rolled on the ground, damaging the shrubs, including a daisy plant not common in New Zealand. Control samples from the scene and samples from the victim and the suspect's clothing all contained large amounts of the daisy pollen and the same combination of other pollen types. To collect so much of the insect-pollinated daisy pollen on his clothing, the suspect must have had prolonged contact with the plant and soil beneath it. He was arrested and convicted of sexual assault.

Some of the most interesting forensic palynology cases in which similarities in the composition of pollen assemblages have been used involved pollen evidence from animals in New Zealand—animals of the four-legged kind. These cases were conducted by Dr Dallas Mildenhall of the Institute for Geological and Nuclear Sciences in New Zealand.

The first case that Dallas worked on[14, 15] involved deer. Deer velvet, the thin layer of fur that grows on deer antlers, is harvested from domestic deer in New Zealand and sold on the Asian market, where it's valued for, among other things, its supposed aphrodisiac properties. In 1980 antlers bearing over NZ$2000 of deer velvet were stolen. The antlers were cut from deer herded into a farmer's stockyard, and carried away hidden in large wool bales stolen from a nearby woolshed.

A person found with wool bales full of deer antlers was questioned. He maintained that the antlers were cut from free-ranging deer in native forest and scrubland in which small grassy clearings occurred. Pollen that adheres to the velvet on free-ranging deer will be from vegetation through which the deer roam. The native scrub from which the suspect alleged he collected the antlers contained shrubs that produce large quantities of pollen.

Dallas examined pollen samples from mud in the stock pens where the deer had been herded, and a sample from a wool bale remaining in the woolshed. These control samples provided the basis for comparison with the forensic samples—mud on the inside and outside of the recovered stolen wool bales, and mud on the base of deer antlers found in the suspect's possession. Mud on one of the antlers was mixed with blood, suggesting that the mud and blood arrived there at the same time—when the antler was being cut off or shortly afterwards.

The control samples and the antlers and wool bales in the suspect's possession all contained identical pollen assemblages, each dominated by the pollen of grasses and daisies. This assemblage was from a cultivated grassland, not from a forest and scrubland environment. Also present was pollen from a walnut tree and a wattle tree, both of which grew close to the stockyard. The suspect was found guilty of stealing the antlers.

Thanks to this case and the large body of forensic palynology casework that Dallas Mildenhall has conducted and reported on over the years, New Zealand is now the world leader in forensic palynology. Yes, New Zealand does beat Australia in some things—and there will be no sheep jokes. At least not until after I relate another case that Dallas worked on where animals carried pollen evidence.[16]

This is a case where the fleece from the flock a fleecer fleeced proved that the fleecer had fleeced the flock. For those not familiar with the saying 'He'd take the wool off a sheep's back', fleecing is a term that my generation use to describe the dishonest removal of money from another person. It usually means stealing by trickery or guile rather than stealing by breaking and entering. In this case it was a carefully planned large-scale break and enter.

Three hundred sheep were stolen from a New Zealand farm. A week later another farmer took 350 sheep to be auctioned at a sheep sale. The auctioneer knew of the theft and he knew that the farmer who brought the sheep to be auctioned didn't own a property large enough to support 350 sheep. The farmer claimed that he had bought the sheep a week earlier but he couldn't produce evidence of their purchase. The sheep were impounded by police. Because they had no distinguishing marks, the farmer who lost the sheep (not Bo-Peep) couldn't confirm that the impounded sheep included those stolen from his property.

Small sections of wool were taken from the backs and head area of several sheep and sent for palynological analysis. Control samples were collected from the farm the sheep were stolen from and from the farm owned by the person who put the sheep up for auction. The pollen assemblage from the sheep's wool was found to be similar to that found at the farm where the sheep had been stolen from, but not like that in the control sample from the other farm. The fleecer was caught. Approximately 300 of the 350 sheep he had brought in for sale had been stolen.

When I was a farmer's daughter we had a tool that clipped out a section of a sheep's ear to distinguish our sheep from other people's sheep. Later, coloured tags clipped onto the ear became fashionable. Did this stop the sheep rustlers? No. I have vivid memories of being rudely awakened from a deep sleep in the back of the car on the way home from a monthly movie at the local town hall. So much for dreams of Cliff Richard and wanting to look like Sandra Dee. Expletives were issuing from my father's mouth that he was forbidden to utter in front of wee children. As he turned into our front gate he saw a light in a paddock alongside the road ahead. This was our paddock and there were no gates in the fence. By the time we checked the fence and found where it had been cut, the truck bearing our sheep was long gone.

Wool, fur, hair and anything made of woven fibres are wonderful pollen traps for forensic pollen analysis. Bryant and Mildenhall[16] report a case in which pollen from rope was used to help solve a murder. A man was found hanged in his barn. He left no suicide note and police suspected foul play. Five people would benefit from the man's death but there was no evidence to suspect one person above the others. The rope the man hung from was different from rope found in his barn. Did the murderer supply his own rope? The rope was sent for pollen analysis and found to contain pollen from vegetables. One of the five suspects grew and sold a variety of vegetable crops. This was not enough to convict the person but it narrowed down the list of suspects. Police put the suspect under surveillance and finally gathered enough evidence to arrest him for murder.

One of the most famous and fascinating cases that involved analysing pollen from woven fabric to determine where something came from is the investigation into the authenticity of the Shroud of Turin.

The Shroud of Turin is a 4.3 x 1.1-metre piece of linen cloth on which a faint image of a man's face and body can be seen. There are various lines of evidence, including blood samples, that suggest that the image is of a man who was crucified. Many believe this is the shroud that was wrapped around the body of Christ after his crucifixion; others believe it's a medieval forgery. Scientists first examined the Shroud at the end of the nineteenth century, and research and debate on its authenticity continue today. Historically, it is alleged that the Shroud was taken from the Holy Land to Constantinople in Turkey and then, in the 1350s it was taken from Turkey to France. The first documented history of the Shroud is from 1352 AD, when it arrived in France. But pollen from the Shroud indicates an earlier history in the Middle East.

Pollen was first collected from the Shroud in 1973 by Dr Max Frei,[17] then head of the Scientific Service of the Criminal Police of Zurich, Switzerland. Some of his previous police work was based on pollen and, while testifying at the Turin Commission of Investigation that photographs of the Shroud taken some years before were authentic, he asked for permission to collect dust samples from the Shroud.

Frei pressed 5-centimetre sections of transparent sticky tape onto the Shroud, lifted them off and mounted them onto glass microscope slides for microscopic examination. He found hundreds of pollen grains on the tapes and compared them with reference pollen collected from plants in Israel, Turkey, Cyprus, France and Italy. Only a few pollen grains were from typical European plants found in Italy and France. Most of the pollen was from plants that grow in different parts of Israel, in nearby Turkey, and the western Mediterranean. Thirty-three per cent of the pollen grains were from *Gundelia tournefortii*, a prickly tumbleweed (thorn) restricted to the Middle East. Among other pollen types, Frei also reported pollen from Rock Rose and a bean caper plant, *Zygophyllum dumosum*, that would later help other investigations of the Shroud. From the natural distribution of plants represented in the pollen assemblage Frei concluded that the Shroud originated in the Middle East in an area near the Dead Sea and Palestine, and that it had travelled through Turkey to France and Italy. He collected further tapes from the Shroud in 1978 but didn't finish examining them before his death in 1983.

In 1988 radiocarbon dating, commonly expressed as carbon-14 or 14^{C}, of linen strands from the Shroud produced a date of 1325 AD, strangely coincident with the first documented history of the Shroud. Sceptics declared the Shroud a thirteenth–fourteenth century forgery, and because Max Frei wasn't a recognised palynologist, his research and findings were not taken seriously.

In the year that Max Frei died, a German physicist, Oswald Scheuermann, noticed flower-like images in enhanced photographs of the Shroud. He conducted experiments and concluded that these images were made by corona discharge—the discharge of radiation from a surface charged with static electricity. That is, where the plant material touched the cloth it lost electrons to the cloth and left faint halo-like images of the outline of the plant material on the cloth. Scheuermann reported his findings to Professor Alan Whanger of Duke University in North Carolina and his wife Mary Whanger.

The Whangers saw these faint images of plant material for themselves on the Shroud in 1985. Over the following decade they enhanced black and white photographs of the Shroud taken in 1931 and detected hundreds of images of flowers, buds, leaves, fruit and stems around the head and on the chest area of the image of the figure of a man on the Shroud. Tentatively, they identified 28 of the plant images as being from plants that grew in Israel.

In 1995 the Whangers enlisted the help of a well-respected Israeli botanist, Dr Avinoam Danin, to confirm their identifications of plants in the Shroud images. Danin was impressed. He verified their work and identified other plants represented by the images. Of particular interest was the image of a flower of the thorn *Gundelia tournefortii* near the right shoulder of the figure on the Shroud, the same place from which Frei had taken a tape that contained numerous *G. tournefortii* pollen grains.

The Whangers had acquired Max Frei's pollen tapes and Danin took them back to Israel in the hope that Dr Uri Baruch, an expert on Israeli palynology, would examine them. Baruch had publicly taken a stand against Frei's findings, but on examining the tapes he changed his opinion. Like Frei, Baruch found that almost one-third of the pollen grains on the tapes were from the thorn *Gundelia tournefortii*.

During another visit to the Whangers, Danin identified leaves and flowers of bean caper plants, *Zygophyllum dumosum*, in the image of a bouquet on the chest area of the figure of a man on the Shroud. At that time Danin didn't know that Frei had reported pollen of *Z. dumosum* on the Shroud tapes. Similarly, an image of a bouquet of Rock Roses was found near the left cheek of the figure. Frei had found Rock Rose pollen on the tapes too.

Although pollen and images from many other plants that grow in the Middle East have been recognised on the Shroud, the independent identification of both pollen and images of *Gundelia tournefortii* and *Zygophyllum dumosum* are the most significant. The thorn *G. tournefortii* is insect pollinated and flowers from February to May. Such great numbers of pollen from this species could only have arrived on the Shroud from a flower being placed on it. *Zygophyllum dumosum* is restricted to Israel, western Jordan and Sinai, and its northernmost distribution occurs between Jerusalem and Jericho.[18] The natural distributions of *G. tournefortii* and *Z. dumosum* overlap in two small areas, both in the Holy Land. From studying distribution grids of all the plants identified by pollen or images, Danin reported that the area the Shroud may have originated from is 10–20 kilometres east and west of Jerusalem.

The Whangers, Danin, Baruch and others have plenty of ammunition for the sceptics. The documented history of the Shroud shows that since 1352 AD it hasn't left Europe. If the similar carbon-14 date for the age of the Shroud is correct, how did so many pollen grains and images of plants from the Middle East come to be on the Shroud? The carbon-14 dating has since been discounted. The linen threads that were dated are chemically different from most of the Shroud linen. Was this younger thread used for mending the Shroud when it first arrived in France, or before it was taken from Constantinople?

Are the images of plant material on the Shroud artefacts or 'faces in the clouds' as one sceptic put it? They could be, but it's unlikely. After examining the pollen and image evidence, even the aforementioned sceptic agreed the images may be authentic. Some images can be seen on the Shroud without the aid of photographic enhancement, and the same images can be seen in photographs of the Shroud taken in 1898 and 1978—eighty years apart and with different cameras, films and developing methods.

The two independent botanical methods, palynology and the analysis of the halo-like images left by coronal discharge, show that plants were placed on the Shroud. Pollen analysis narrowed down the area from which the Shroud originated and determined the time of year when the pollen arrived on it. None of this proves that the Shroud was used to cover the body of Christ. I'm not an adherent of traditional religion, but the abundant presence of pollen from the thorn *Gundelia tournefortii* and its image near the shoulder of the figure on the Shroud does provoke thought. This species is not an ornamental and is unlikely to have been used in a floral tribute.

In Search of Pollen

Pollen isn't hard to find. You can walk into a garden, find a flower, and inside there will be pollen, as long as the bees haven't got there first. If you want to see what this yellow powder really looks like you can put it under a microscope. But if the pollen is straight from a flower you won't see the fine details of its surface and wall structure that you can see in the photographs of pollen in this book.

A pollen grain fresh from a flower is like a jelly blob with symmetry. Its finer structural details will usually be obscured by a film of oily material (lipids) covering its outer surface, and by the fluid (cytoplasm) inside it that contains the two male sex cells. To see pollen grains clearly under a microscope, palynologists first have to chemically remove this 'goo' to leave only its non-living wall, the structure that we actually study. This isn't unlike removing the skin, flesh and internal organs of an animal from its bony skeleton.

There are similar problems when it comes to finding dispersed pollen—pollen in soil, rocks, dirt, dust and water samples. The pollen fraction of a sample has to be isolated from its mineral components (e.g. sand and clay) and other small particles of organic matter (e.g. fragments of leaves, roots, wood and insects).

Fresh pollen samples and those containing dispersed pollen go through a variety of chemical and physical treatments before they are microscopically examined. Collectively these procedures are called palynological preparation or processing, or just processing for short. The aim of processing is to reduce the size of the sample by removing as much of the unwanted organic matter and minerals as possible, retaining only the pollen-sized organic matter. How pollen samples are prepared and in what order the procedures are carried out may differ slightly from one laboratory to another.

To mothers, working in a laboratory is like working in a kitchen—lots of cooking and washing up. To children, a laboratory is a fun place. On the occasions when my children came into the laboratory with me while I was working on my PhD, they returned home with the odd bit of disposable equipment—their reward for being good. Fine rubber gloves were blown up into five-fingered balloons or filled with water and the fingers pricked to form a pretend cow's udder. Plastic pipettes were used for mini water pistols or to drink their milk with, and small plastic and glass vials with screw tops were filled with beads, bugs, and other treasures. Caroline still has these lined along her bookshelf.

My introduction to laboratory work when I started my PhD in 1989 had involved two mornings in the palynology technician's laboratory learning the basic procedures of palynology preparation. I understood rock chemistry on paper but had no formal chemistry background or practical experience, and was terrified of being left to work on my own. But I was, and by the end of the first two days alone in the student laboratory I had cleaned everything in sight, several times. On the third day I could no longer put off the inevitable. Walking up from the car park I had syncopated my steps with a mantra: 'I can do it, I can do it, I can do it'. And do it I did. But only because I had walked into the laboratory purposefully and devoid of emotion and worked like a robot—completely detached. Today, any robotic detachment is due to boredom with routine, not fear. However, it is not wise to become complacent about working in a laboratory because the chemicals they contain are dangerous and must be used with care.

The most dangerous chemical used to prepare palynology samples is hydrofluoric acid (HF). It digests silicate minerals such as quartz and clays, but if it is spilt on 2% or more of the body surface and not treated quickly, it can cause death. Fluoride ions in HF permeate the skin quickly and react with calcium ions in our cells to form calcium fluoride, an insoluble precipitate. This locks up the calcium needed for, among other things, blood clotting, muscle contraction and a normal heartbeat. Not a friendly acid.

Where I work today, HF procedures are carried out in a different laboratory to other pollen preparations and users undergo training. We wear heavy yellow plastic suits ('banana suits') with a hood, gum boots, two pairs of special gloves and a visor helmet that angles under the chin to prevent fumes from rising up inside it (Plate 15). We treat the samples with HF under a fume extractor in a fume cupboard. The HF laboratory is not a place to work in alone. If something goes wrong someone else needs to be there to call for help, administer treatment if necessary and help clean up.

Some of the procedures for preparing palynology samples involve the use of a centrifuge (Plates 15–17). A centrifuge works on the principle of centrifugal force and is a smaller and faster version of the gravity-defying rides at theme parks and fairs. As a child at the local agricultural show I recall a spinning cylindrical room with no roof that spun so fast its standing occupants were flattened up against the wall. From the viewing platform above I watched it spin, fascinated by the embarrassed young women in gathered skirts and blousey blouses that clung to them revealing every bump in their bodies. Attempts to cover their most prominent bumps were met with hoots from their male companions. Recalling this, I let my young children ride in the Gravitron at Dreamworld on the Gold Coast in southern Queensland. Their clinging clothes would reveal little, and modesty was yet to enter their vocabulary. Standing around the inside wall of a spinning machine and getting giddy could do them no harm. But when I climbed up to the viewing platform I was horrified. There was Caroline, my then six-year-old, halfway up the wall, upside down. So much for standing. Centrifugal force overrides the force of gravity.

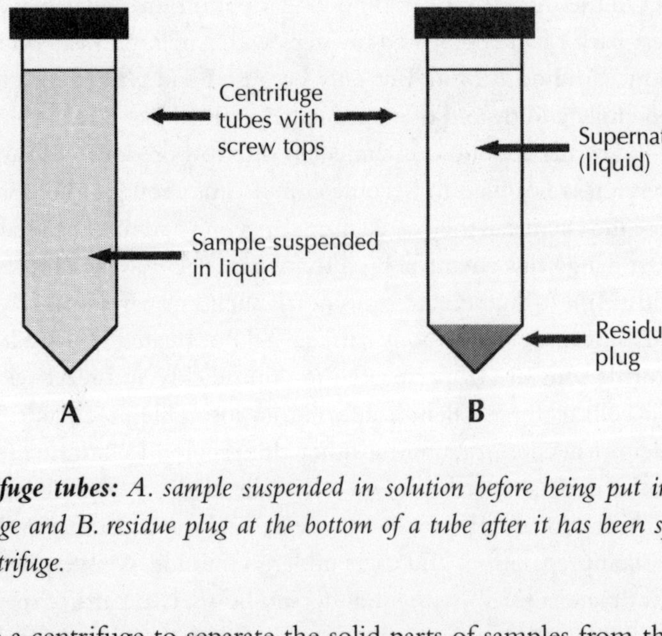

Centrifuge tubes: *A. sample suspended in solution before being put into the centrifuge and B. residue plug at the bottom of a tube after it has been spun in the centrifuge.*

We use a centrifuge to separate the solid parts of samples from the various chemical solutions and water rinses they go through during pollen preparation. The samples, mixed in the solution or in water, are placed into plastic test tubes (centrifuge tubes) with screw tops. The tubes are placed upright into holders in the centrifuge (Plate 16) and spun at about 3500 revolutions a minute for several minutes. As the centrifuge speeds up the tubes become horizontal, their bases forming the outer part of the spinning circle of tubes

(Plate 17). The solids are forced to the base of the tubes and form a 'residue plug'. When the centrifuge stops, the tubes are removed and the liquid on top, the supernatant, is poured off and discarded. The diagram opposite illustrates what the sample in a centrifuge tube looks like before and after it has been centrifuged.

Fresh pollen from a flower and dispersed pollen in soil samples and Quaternary sedimentary rocks undergo a process called acetolysis (Table 1). Acetolysis removes much of the unwanted organic matter in a sample. It digests cellulose, the major component of plant cell walls, and the outer lipids and inner cytoplasm of the pollen grains. However, it doesn't harm the pollen 'skeleton' because, as mentioned earlier, the pollen walls are made of a tough, acid-resistant material called sporopollenin.

The acetolysis mixture is made from acetic anhydride and sulphuric acid. Acetic anhydride, as its name suggests, is anhydrous; that is, it doesn't mix with water. But it does mix with acetic acid, which in turn mixes with acetic anhydride. For this reason samples are rinsed several times in acetic acid to remove any water in them before they're boiled in the acetolysis mixture. They are rinsed again afterwards with acetic acid to remove traces of acetic anhydride before the sample goes back into water.

Table 1. Acetolysis: Chemical preparation of fresh pollen for microscopic analysis

Chemicals/procedures in order of use	What the procedure does to the pollen sample
Acetic acid	Rinsing the sample in this several times removes all water.
Acetolysis—mixture of acetic anhydride and sulphuric acid	Boiling the pollen sample in this mixture: • removes the pollen contents (cytoplasm) and oily substances (lipids) on the outside of pollen grains, and • destroys unwanted plant material in the sample.
Acetic acid	Rinsing the sample with this several times removes all the acetolysis mixture so the sample can go back into water.

Acetolysis doesn't take long, but it's smelly. Acetic acid is like strong vinegar. Acetolysis is not usually performed on samples from sedimentary rocks that are more than 2 million years old (pre-Quaternary). The cytoplasm in the pollen they contain has long gone and the unwanted organic material in these samples can be removed by other chemical treatments.

Soil, dirt and dust samples are usually demineralised before they are acetolysed (Table 2). Hydrochloric acid (HCl) is used to remove carbonate minerals (e.g. limestone), and hydrofluoric acid (HF) removes the silicate minerals (e.g. quartz and clays). When HF reacts with silicate minerals it forms other compounds (fluorosilicates) that must be removed from the sample with HCl.

Table 2. Chemical preparation of soil and Quaternary sedimentary rock samples for pollen analysis

Chemicals/procedures in order of use	What the procedure does to the pollen sample
Hydrochloric acid (HCl)	Removes carbonate minerals (e.g. those that make up limestone).
Hydrofluoric acid (HF)	Removes silicate minerals (e.g. quartz and clays).
Hydrochloric acid	Removes the fluoride gel formed by the reaction between hydrofluoric acid and the silicate minerals.
Acetolysis	Removes unwanted organic material. Used for soil and Quaternary sediments. Another chemical is used for geologically older samples.
Zinc bromide	A heavy liquid. Used to separate light plant material, including pollen, from heavy plant material and heavy minerals not digested by HCl and HF (e.g. ilmenite).
Sieving	Concentrates the sample by removing organic matter larger than, and smaller than, pollen grains.

After the minerals are removed, all that should remain is organic material and heavy minerals that are not digested by HCl and HF. To further concentrate the pollen fraction of the sample, heavy minerals and heavy plant material such as leaf tissue and large bits of charcoal can be removed by 'heavy liquid separation', and lighter plant fragments larger and smaller than pollen can be removed by sieving with different-sized sieve meshes (sieve meshes can be as small as 1 μm).

For heavy liquid separation the sample is mixed with a liquid that is heavier than water, such as zinc bromide. The sample and a small amount of the heavy liquid are put into a centrifuge tube, mixed well, and spun in the centrifuge. When the tubes come out of the centrifuge the heavy unwanted particles are at the bottom of the tube and the lighter particles, including pollen, float on top of the heavy liquid or are suspended in it. The liquid portion is pipetted (sucked) out of each tube and retained, and the heavy material at the bottom of the tube is discarded or put aside in case it needs to be examined later. The retained heavy liquid with pollen and other fine organic matter suspended in it is then diluted with water so that the suspended material will sink to the bottom of the tubes when they are centrifuged again.

The organic material that remains after a soil or fresh pollen sample has been palynologically processed is called the sample residue. To make a permanent slide of the residue for microscopy, a small drop of it is placed on a glass microscope slide, mixed with a microscope mounting medium (e.g. glycerine jelly, glycerol, silicon oil or a plastic material) and covered with a glass coverslip.

In forensic palynology most soil samples and fresh pollen samples that have to be processed are control samples. These are collected from a crime scene, or a herbarium in the case of pollen reference material. Pollen in the control samples is compared with the pollen assemblages recovered from items the police suspect might be associated with a crime. Police call these items, or samples they have collected from them, exhibits. I call the samples that I process from exhibits forensic samples, to distinguish them from the control samples when I'm processing, and from the original exhibits I received from the police.

Some of the exhibits forensic palynologists have examined in the past include interesting things like intestines, feathers, ink, paint and condoms, but the most common exhibits are clothing, shoes and parts of cars.

Ideally, a palynologist should remove material that might contain pollen from an exhibit. This isn't always possible for large items such as cars, and in some jurisdictions it's not permitted, so police will collect the material from them for pollen analysis by tape-lifting or vacuuming. Because processing a sample for palynology will destroy other evidence such as blood, other body fluids, fibres, hair, soil, paint flakes and gunshot residue, other forensic scientists might work on the tape-lifts or vacuumings first. But in most of the cases I have worked on, the exhibits, or materials collected from them, have either come to me without the need for other scientists to examine them, or one half of the sample has been given to other scientists and I have the other half.

Police give me exhibit samples in sealed, heavy-duty paper exhibit bags. Across the packaging tape used to seal them is a piece of 'evidence tape' signed and dated by the person who last sealed the bag. The next person to open the bag reseals it, puts more evidence tape over the seals, and signs and dates it. When receiving an exhibit bag I sign a document to say that I have received it and walk away with the sealed bag. The evidence tape and hand-over documents are required to maintain the chain of evidence. In other words, they record who has had the exhibit and when they had it to ensure that someone is officially responsible for it at all times. When I walk away with the sealed exhibit bag I also have a copy of the document I signed. This also lists the contents of the bag. Nevertheless, opening exhibit bags in the laboratory is still like opening Christmas presents—they're full of surprises.

Tape-lifts collected by the police are my least favourite samples to work on. A tape-lift sheet is the size of a standard A4 sheet of paper and has a strong adhesive surface protected by a non-adhesive backing sheet. The adhesive surface is pressed firmly onto the surface of the item of interest, lifted off and the backing sheet is replaced to prevent airborne particles from contaminating the tape surface. For palynology, the tape sheets are cut up to fit microscope slides and secured on the slides with double-sided tape. Pollen collected on tape-lifts usually still contains its cytoplasm and lipid coating. This, and the mass of other debris that tape-lifts collect, means that pollen is difficult to find and identify on tape-lifts.

Tape-lifts only collect material on or near the surface of an item; they don't collect pollen grains trapped in the fibres of woven fabric, carpets, hair or fur. Similarly, vacuuming doesn't remove all the pollen. I've found that even after a carpet has been vacuumed several times, as much pollen remains in the carpet as is vacuumed up. My preferred method of removing a sample from fabric, carpet and similar exhibits is to brush, scrape and shake the loose material from them, then wash them in a special solution. Normal washing with washing powder or detergent doesn't remove all pollen.

Washing exhibits is sometimes unpleasant. In a recent case the exhibit bag contained numerous articles of clothing and a pair of shoes. The clothing was very dirty and I was glad of my gloves but wished we had also used masks. It took a day to soak and wash these smelly articles and another day to centrifuge the resulting water to concentrate the solid material washed from them. When the tubes containing the washing water from those dirty clothes came out of the centrifuge, a film of grease and skin cells floated on top of the supernatant. As the water was tipped from the tubes the rising smell of body odour filled the room. No lunch for me that day.

Collecting pollen from some exhibits can be a challenge. When police asked if I could collect pollen from a car air filter, I envisioned a small filter like those we use in the laboratory, and agreed that it could be done. Expecting to collect a tiny exhibit bag, I was surprised to be given a large bag that looked as if it hid a tennis racquet with a fat head. My initial response was to play it cool—walk out with the bag under my arm and worry about what was in it later. Thinking the better of this, I used my womanly wiles to plead ignorance of how an air filter worked. I needed to know where the pollen might collect.

Obligingly, the officers opened the bag and took out a large object like a frying pan with a lid. So much for tennis. Inside was a circular object and behind a metal grid around the middle of this object was a concertina-like cardboard filter. In the laboratory I used every conceivable cutting implement in the tool box to get through the metal to access the cardboard filter. The effort and resulting blisters were worth it. The pollen told a story and I had the satisfaction of pulling apart and rendering completely useless a part of a car. Plate 18 shows the dismantled air filter.

Before removing pollen from exhibits, all aspects of the case that involve the exhibits must be considered. Contamination while removing the pollen samples and from poor laboratory practice are always foremost in a palynologist's mind. What order the samples should be processed in is also important. Decisions on how and when each sample will be processed must be made in light of possible questioning if the case goes to court. For example, if the control samples are processed before the exhibit samples, or on the same day, and incriminating pollen evidence is found in the exhibit samples, it could be suggested that the exhibit samples were accidentally contaminated with material from the control samples. This could be from dirty gloves, glassware or stirring rods, or by accidentally mixing some of the control sample with the exhibit sample. Thinking of all the things that might go wrong and taking steps to prevent them, and the extra work that has to be done to firm up positive evidence if it is found, were things I didn't consider when I was first asked to work on Samantha Hall's case.

The Foundations

During the last three years of my PhD project, 1994–97, Byron Steel and I shared an office at the University of Queensland with several other postgraduate students and a Postdoctoral Fellow. I mostly worked at home on my own microscope and computer, only going in to the university to do laboratory work, electron microscopy and to catch up on gossip. My desk was mine in name only and was invariably covered with the remains of our resident Postdoc's last few meals and ingredients for his next one. Rarely working in the office, I only knew Byron from our 'goss' sessions in there and the evening get-togethers we had as a group every couple of weeks to re-hash the goss and drink red wine.

More than 30 years separated the youngest of our group of five from the oldest, our common ground being the difficulties of postgraduate research and our position at the bottom of the academic hierarchy. I was the second oldest and Byron was the second youngest, at 23. My interaction with this bouncy, outwardly cheerful, small package of a person was more maternal than academic. His choirboy face and cheeky grin framed by a shock of fair hair would melt any mother's heart. Sadly, this young man's mother was not his favourite person. She had bestowed on him a poetic name and small stature, and his desire to formally change his given name was a constant point of contention between them. He would prefer we called him Steel. It was more manly. We complied—mostly. To his chagrin we progressed Steel to Seal, then by association called him Sammy, as in Sammy Seal, because of his tendency to clap his hands and bounce on the spot when he was excited.

As mentioned previously, Steel's PhD was partially funded by a police grant to document pollen assemblages from different vegetation communities. He was starting out in palynology and I had been in the field for over 15 years. Steel was quite secretive about his work, so I was surprised when he asked if I could do scanning electron microscopy (SEM) on samples from a murder case he was working on. It was early March 1997 and my PhD thesis was due to be completed by the end of June. Being way behind schedule I had little time to spare.

'But it's only a couple of samples, and they shouldn't take too long. Maybe an hour or so', he said, with a look that belied such a time frame.

Steel was good at pleading. The little boy lost look got me every time.

'Okay then', I sighed. 'What's the case and what exactly do you want me to do?'

'Well, last year a woman's body was found among flowering wattle shrubs at the end of Hastings Street in Noosa, but she actually lived in Gympie. Police found her car in Gympie and there was a wattle flower in it. They think the murderer may have used the victim's car to drive her body to Noosa', he explained.

'So police want to know if the wattle flower is from Noosa?' I enquired.

'Yeah. Police gave me three flower samples from the crime scene. I've looked at their pollen and compared it with pollen from the flower found in the car. It all looks the same', he said despondently.

'So what's the problem?' I asked. Surely that was good news.

'Yesterday I took the plant samples to the herbarium to be identified, and there are two different wattle species at Noosa', he explained. 'If I can't tell the difference between the pollen from those two species, how can I tell what species the flower in the car is, or where the pollen on his clothes came from?' he said with a hint of frustration.

'Whose clothes?' I asked. The plot was thickening.

'One of the suspects, the chief suspect. Police gave me tape-lifts from his clothes and I've found some wattle pollen on them', he replied.

'Well done', I congratulated him.

'But I can't tell if they're the same or different to the pollen from Noosa', he said, raising his voice at the end of the sentence to emphasise his dilemma.

Wattles are insect pollinated and all things being equal, the pollen from each species should be different. 'Can we go back to the beginning?' I asked. He nodded, and I continued. 'The two species at Noosa…you say their pollen is the same. Do you mean they're the same size with the same ornamentation and wall structure?'

'I don't know. I can't see them very well', he admitted.

'You processed them, didn't you?' I queried.

He looked blank, and then realised what I meant. 'You mean did I acetolyse them?'

'Yes. You should see the structure really well if you've done that', I noted.

'No, I haven't. I can't. They have to be compared with pollen on the tape-lifts, and the tape-lifts can't be acetolysed', he asserted.

At first I didn't understand Steel's last statement. Then I realised that if the tape-lifts were acetolysed, the chemicals might destroy the adhesive on the tape and the pollen—the evidence—might be lost. He was probably right about that. As for not processing pollen from flowers on the control plant specimens collected at the crime scene, I suspected he meant that to compare it with the unprocessed pollen on the tape-lifts, pollen from the control flowers should also be left unprocessed.

Pollen that hadn't been acetolysed couldn't be examined in the SEM I used. There was probably a way around that. A way to clear the pollen on the tape-lift of its cytoplasm without dislodging the pollen from the tape could surely be found. But I needed to know more about the samples and the case before making any suggestions.

'Did you tell police you were going to ask me to help you?' I asked Steel.

'Yes. They said they'd contact you about it', he replied.

'All right', I said resignedly. 'Tell me the whole story—what samples the police have given you and what you have done with them so far. Then I'll see what I can do.'

Sammy was relieved. As we walked to the coffee shop on the other side of campus the story unfolded.

In early September the previous year, several weeks after the victim's body was found, police had given Steel tape-lift samples from the victim's and a suspect's clothing, tape-lift and vacuum filter samples from the victim's car, a wattle flower found in the front driver's side of the victim's car and plant control samples with flowers on from the wattle plants growing at the Noosa crime scene (Table 3). His initial task was to determine if there was any wattle pollen on the clothing tapes and in the vacuum filter samples from the car. If there was, he was to compare it with pollen from the flower found in the car and with pollen from the flowers collected at the crime scene.

Table 3. Samples the police first gave Steel to examine	
Forensic samples (exhibits)	**Control samples**
Numerous tape-lift sheets from: • the victim's clothing • the chief suspect's clothing and • the victim's car. Wattle flower from victim's car. Vacuuming samples from victim's car.	Three samples of wattle plant material collected from the Noosa crime scene.

Clothing belonging to the chief suspect had been collected by police on the evening of the day the body of Samantha Hall had been found. After he had been interviewed, a 'posse' of seven to eight police officers had escorted him back to his room in the Mt Pleasant Hotel. The police presence had been primarily to examine his room for any evidence that might be there, but was also to protect him from the potential 'lynch mob' that had been angrily brewing in the bar below. Samantha's friends were rallying around another person in Samantha's life who police also considered to be a 'person of interest'. Police use this term, or POI for short, to refer to people they suspect may have been involved in a crime.

A number of articles of clothing, including those found hanging on the washing line, had been collected from the chief suspect that Saturday night. Back at Scientific Section in Brisbane, tape-lifts had been taken from three pairs of jeans, several shirts, a pullover, socks and underpants. It was tape-lifts from this clothing that Steel examined first. He put a light red stain on the tape-lift sheets to highlight the pollen and other plant material among the fibres and soil. Then he cut up the sheets to fit microscope slides and attached each piece of tape to a slide.

Over the next week Steel spent many tedious hours examining the tape-lift slides. He found several wattle pollen grains and fragments of grains on tape-lifts from one pair of jeans and one shirt belonging to the chief suspect. He returned all the other exhibits to the police except the tape-lift slides containing wattle pollen grains, the flower from the car, the vacuum filter sample from the front driver's side of the victim's car, and the control flower samples from the crime scene (Table 4).

Table 4. Samples Steel retained for further examination and those he returned to police a week after he first received them	
Samples retained	**Samples returned to police**
Tape-lifts from the jeans and shirt of the chief suspect. Wattle flower the victim's car. Vacuum filter sample from the front driver's side of the victim's car.	Tape-lifts from other clothing belonging to the chief suspect, and from the victim's clothing. Vacuum filter samples and samples from parts of the victim's car other than the front driver's side.

Because the wattle pollen Steel found on the tape-lifts was unprocessed and difficult to see among the fibres and dust particles, he sought ways of dissolving the tape adhesive to gently release the pollen from the tape. Good thinking. Manually lifting the grains off the adhesive would risk their being broken or lost. None of the solvents he tried on the tapes worked. The adhesive either remained intact or agglutinated into a gooey mass that enveloped any debris on the tape. If pollen had been on the tape it too would have disappeared in the gooey mass. Steel was at a loss what to do next. As he related this saga I wondered how other forensic scientists examined pollen on tape-lifts. Surely there must be an easier way.

After examining the clothing tape-lifts, Steel had processed the vacuum filter sample from the victim's car to remove all the carbonate and silicate minerals (dust and sand grains). Now all that remained of the original sample was a tangled mass of organic matter. Microscopic examination of a slide made from a small drop of this organic residue yielded only one wattle pollen grain, and he concluded that the sample showed little promise of providing evidence.

Contrary to Steel's bleak outlook, I was excited about the wattle pollen grain in the vacuum filter sample. If the sample was acetolysed and the pollen fraction concentrated, I believed a rich pollen assemblage would be found in the sample—pollen from the car's everyday use, and more wattle pollen if it was indeed there. Steel was tentative, worried that important pollen grains might be lost or broken up during acetolysis and he took some convincing that wattle pollen would survive intact. His fears were not unreasonable because, as noted previously, wattle pollen is a composite grain (polyad) of 10–16 individual pollen grains (monads). But from my years of experience in palynology I knew that most wattle pollen grains didn't break up during acetolysis.

After examining the demineralised vacuum filter sample, Steel looked at pollen from the control flowers collected from the crime scene and from the flower found inside the victim's car. Police had taken flowers from three wattle plants they thought might be different species. If they were different species Steel hoped their pollen would look different. He took fresh pollen from each control flower and mounted it in glycerine jelly on microscope slides.

Pollen from each sample looked the same. Had the police been mistaken? Was there only one species of wattle at the crime scene, not two or three?

To further complicate Steel's task there was the question of where the suspect had been in Gympie. Were there any flowering wattle plants there that he may have brushed against? To determine this, Detectives Paul Zohn and Kim Cavell accompanied Steel as he conducted a botanical survey of the areas in Gympie where the suspect alleged he had been on the days leading up to the crime. They surveyed 10 metres either side of the areas of interest: near the victim's home, near the Mt Pleasant Hotel where the suspect lived and the nightclub car park in which the victim's car had been found.

No wattle bushes were found near the hotel or the nightclub but three small wattle shrubs were found off to the side of a path, and near Samantha Hall's home there were numerous small wattle shrubs. None of the plants was flowering. Steel collected small sections from each type of wattle.

Plant groups are primarily differentiated by their reproductive structures—flowers, and fruiting bodies such as banksia cones and gumnuts. Collectors usually sample a 30–40 centimetre section that includes leaves, stems and, if possible, flowers or fruit. If reproductive structures are not present, other features, such as the shape of the leaves, their arrangement on the stem and the plant's habit (tree, shrub, herb or vine) may be used for identification. But some wattle species are difficult to identify without their flowers.

The Gympie plant samples and those that police had collected from the Noosa crime scene were taken to the Brisbane Herbarium to be formally identified. To Steel's dismay the botanist identified two species at Noosa: *Acacia saligna* and *A. sophorae* (now known as *A. longifolia* subsp. *sophorae*, but referred to here as *A. sophorae*). But there was also good news. The wattle species at Gympie were different from those at Noosa. All but one of the Gympie plant samples were from *A. aulacocarpa* or *A. falcata*. There was only one sample the botanist couldn't positively identify without its flowers. She suggested it might be *A. holosericea* or *A. cowleana*, but she was uncertain if it was one of these species or an entirely different species.

Steel investigated the flowering periods of the wattle species from Gympie to determine if they were flowering in late August, when the murder occurred.

He found that *Acacia aulacocarpa* flowers from February to April and *A. falcata* from May to July, ruling out these plants as a source of the flower found in the victim's car.

That left the single sample the botanist had suggested might be either *Acacia cowleana* or *A. holosericea. Acacia cowleana* flowers from May to August/ September and *A. holosericea* from June to August. The plant this sample came from was the only one of its kind found during the botanical survey at Gympie. A young shrub with only one long branch, it was found among a group of larger *A. falcata* shrubs. If it was one of the species the botanist had suggested, then in late August it was at the end of its flowering period. It was unlikely, although not impossible, that this solitary shrub, which was set well back from a pathway, was the source of the wattle pollen grains found on the suspect's clothing and the flower in the victim's car. In summary, it was highly unlikely that any of the wattle plants identified at Gympie had anything to do with the case.

Steel had also investigated whether the two species growing at the Noosa crime scene, *Acacia sophorae* and *A. saligna*, were also likely to be growing in Gympie. He found that *A. sophorae* grew in coastal sand dunes and its northernmost natural occurrence was south of Noosa. *Acacia saligna* was also not native to the Noosa area and its natural distribution was coastal areas south of Noosa. Both species had been planted in the area where the victim's body had been found to stabilise the new sand spit, and would not grow in Gympie. Police had already established that the victim hadn't driven her car to Noosa while *A. sophorae* and *A. saligna* were flowering. The suspect alleged that he hadn't been near any wattle plants except those growing in Gympie.

I now had the story so far. Steel summarised his problems.

'I can't tell the difference between pollen of different wattle species so I can't compare it with pollen on the tapes and in the vacuum filter. I can't get the pollen grains off the tapes and the vacuum filter sample is so full of other garbage I can't find much pollen. I'm stumped. Do you think you could do SEM on the two species from Noosa to see if you can tell them apart?' he asked.

'Yes, but only if the pollen is processed', I replied. 'If it's not processed we won't see the surface of it clearly. Besides, the pollen contents will heat up under the electron beam and the grains will expand, and even explode. It's fun to watch but not good for the microscope', I explained.

'But we have to use unprocessed pollen', Steel emphasised.

I drifted off into my 'think tank', that faraway place that frustrates my children when they want an answer to a question now, not in a minute or three. Again, Steel was referring to his belief that in order to make an effective comparison of the unprocessed pollen on the tape-lifts with pollen from the plant samples collected at the crime scene, he would have to leave the crime scene pollen unprocessed. I respected his caution but, for two reasons, didn't agree with him. Firstly, I believed that there must be some way to process the pollen on the tape. Secondly, looking at unprocessed pollen is like looking at a poorly focussed photograph of people—the fine features can't be seen. But if we know what a person looks like it is easy to identify them in an unfocussed photo. This also applies to pollen. It is easier to identify unprocessed pollen if we know what it looks like when it is processed.

I slowly came back from the faraway place. Steel had used 'I can't' four times when summarising his problems, and the detective in me had been working overtime while he protested. Not the kind of detective that deals with criminal cases, but the detective side of mothers. The detective mother who knows that you took your shoes off at school because your feet are dirty or that you haven't had a shower because the soap isn't wet. I inherited this from my mother. She was, and still is, an ace sleuth. In my early years I thought she was magical and could fly from our farm to my school and spy on me from above.

I began to question Steel like I did my own children when they said 'I can't'.

'Can I have a look at the flower samples from Noosa and the flower from the car?' I asked.

'Not now, they're in at Scientific Section. But I can bring them in on Monday', he replied.

'Is there enough left to process part of them?' I queried.

'Not much.'

'Well that's easily fixed', I asserted. 'Now you know what species are at Noosa you can collect reference pollen from those species on sheets in the herbarium and process it. Then you should be able to see clearly in light microscopy if their pollen really is the same', I explained. 'You shouldn't need SEM.'

'I didn't think of that', he said, brightening up. Then he frowned again. 'But I can't compare processed pollen with pollen on the tapes', he persisted.

'Well I believe you can, but you could also try processing the bit of tape the pollen is on', I suggested.

'How can I do that and not lose the pollen?' he asked.

'I could probably find a way', I said, with more bravado than confidence. During my PhD research I had devised simple ways to conduct palynology procedures that traditionally took weeks to do. Admittedly, they took me months to perfect and I'd picked many brilliant minds on the way, but the 'pollen on tape' problem was simple by comparison.

Steel's shoulders lifted with relief: all was not lost and at last he had someone to talk to about the case. I understand now where he was coming from.

Even with the experience I now have, there are still times when the weight of responsibility makes me tentative, indecisive and overly cautious. Forensic work can be very lonely if there are no peers around to discuss it with.

'What about the vacuum filter sample?' he asked. 'I've removed the minerals but how can I get rid of all the really fine organic material and the large plant particles and fibres without acetolysing the sample?' We were back to the not acetolysing problem again. I explained my unfocussed photograph theory and suggested that we only needed to process half of the sample; the rest could be kept in case it was necessary to look for unprocessed wattle pollen grains. Success. He was finally convinced.

'Can I have a look at it to see what can be done? Maybe take it home?' I asked.

'Sure. It's in at Scientific Section with the other samples', Steel replied. 'I'll bring it in on Monday with the rest of the samples.'

'That would be good', I said. 'Let's write down all the things you have to bring in.' I tore a page from the back of my diary and jotted down:

1. Wattle flower samples from the Noosa scene.
2. Wattle flower from the victim's car.
3. Vacuum filter sample from the front driver's side of the victim's car.
4. Tape-lift slides from the chief suspect's clothing.

During our discussion I found myself being more and more drawn in. It seemed electron microscopy wasn't the only thing Steel needed help with; it was the whole case. He'd done all he was capable of doing and had admitted to police that he couldn't provide them with the information they wanted, but could recommend someone with more experience to help him or continue from where he left off. I suspected he favoured passing the whole lot over to me. It was now six months since he had received the material and he'd spent much of that time hoping it would all go away. Police wanted a result as soon as possible.

The work Steel had done so far was substantial and provided a good foundation on which to build. I soon forgot that I had little time to spare as I thought about ways to process and analyse the samples. What was an insurmountable barrier to Steel was a challenge to me. I was sucked in but refused to commit to working on the case until I had talked to my children and the police had contacted me to confirm Steel's request.

Steel agreed to contact the police that afternoon and they would phone me the following day, Friday. We agreed to meet on Monday afternoon in our office for him to give me the samples. I had the weekend to ponder whether I would agree to work on the case or not.

As we walked back to our office the bounce in Steel's step and his cheeky smile returned. He had a list of things to do and the possibility that someone else might take responsibility for the rest of the case work. Mission accomplished.

If Dogs Could Talk

Over the weekend I considered Steel's proposition and the subsequent phone call from the police on Friday to confirm that they wished me to work on Samantha Hall's case. I had to consider that my thesis was officially due to be completed in less than four months and that I was already way behind schedule. I also had to consider my family. How might they be affected by my taking on this case? In the light of my conversation with the police, I also had to bear in mind what might happen if I refused to work on the case.

Friday night and Saturday were busy with the girls' usual extracurricular activities and the weekend shopping, washing and cleaning, so there was little time to ponder the pros and cons of taking on the case in any great depth. It wasn't until the early hours of Sunday morning while I was at work that there was time to think about it rationally. The work I was paid to do wasn't mentally taxing so I looked forward to these few hours each week. It was my reflection time. But on this Sunday I had some serious thinking to do. I started by pondering why Steel needed help with the case.

The type of palynology Steel did was very general in comparison with the kind of palynology I did. He grouped pollen from the same plant family together and rarely had to distinguish between pollen from different species. Using untreated pollen, it was not surprising that he couldn't distinguish between pollen from the two wattle species. Even if he did acetolyse the samples, would he be any the wiser? Probably not. It had taken me years to develop an 'eye' for the subtle structural differences between pollen of closely related species. Steel had come up with a blank, and if I didn't take on the case police might believe palynology was of no use to them now, or in the future. This would be sad because I knew of international colleagues who conducted forensic palynology with great success and who were struggling to promote its wider use. I would be letting my colleagues down if I refused to take on the case, and police would have no evidence to prove or disprove that their suspect had committed the murder. Steel was stressed out, the police were agitating for a result, and the victim's family were keen for closure after so many months.

As I drove home from work that Sunday morning in 1997 there seemed to be more reasons *for* me to use my skills to work on the case than there were *against* it. At dinner that night I broached the subject with my daughters.

'How would you feel if I were to work on a murder case?' I asked.

'That'd be coooool, Mum', Belinda said, jigging excitedly in her seat.

'What about you Caroline?' I asked my younger daughter.

'Yeah, it's OK with me, Mum, as long as you want to do it', said Caroline, ever the quiet and thoughtful diplomat.

'Wow, wait 'til my friends hear about this!' exclaimed Belinda, gulping down her last mouthful and heading for the phone.

'Oh no you don't', I cautioned her. 'Sit back down and let's talk about this.' Reluctantly Belinda sat down, one leg to the side of her chair, ready for a quick getaway to the phone.

'You are *not* to tell any of your friends', I warned. 'We're a team. We're making this decision together and if you talk about it, you'll be letting the team down', I explained. The girls nodded seriously, Caroline glaring at Belinda as if to say, 'Don't you dare say anything'.

'All right, I promise', Belinda said with a resigned shrug.

That resolved, I pondered my own reservations about working on the case while I cleaned up the kitchen. Steel hadn't told his supervisor he was working on the case, and he had asked me, another student, to help him with it. Would my qualifications be as credible in court as those of a person who already had a PhD? I reasoned that my years of working as a palynologist and my experience in electron microscopy should carry me through, and that Steel's decision not to involve his supervisor was his problem. I suspected their relationship was strained but didn't want to pry too much. Tension between postgraduate students and their supervisors is not uncommon, and usually stems from their differing expectations of each other. Poor Sammy Steel was stressed; he was my friend, and of course I would help him.

On Monday I met Steel as arranged and told him I was prepared to take responsibility for the pollen preparation and analysis still to be done on the case. But there were conditions. He was to collect the pollen reference samples from the herbarium and work with me in the laboratory where he could see what I was doing and why I did it. If he was serious about becoming a forensic palynologist, he needed the experience for future case work. I would also appreciate his advice on dealing with the police and forensic palynology in general. He had friends and family in the police force and had researched international forensic palynology cases for his PhD project. We were both novices. He in palynology and me in forensic science. Together we would bumble through.

As promised, Steel had collected the flower specimens, tape-lift slides and vacuum filter sample from Scientific Section. First he handed me a large vial about the size of a small jam jar. It was half full. This was the vacuum filter sample from the front driver's side of the victim's car. He had already removed the carbonate and silicate minerals from it using HCl and HF respectively. All that remained was organic matter and minerals not digested by HCl and HF.

I took the vial, shook it, and swirled the contents to see what was in it.

'So what do you think needs to be done to it?' Steel asked.

'It probably needs to be sieved with 150 μm mesh first to remove all the large plant material and fibres', I suggested. 'Then…heavy liquid separation with zinc bromide. That should reduce the sample a lot and it'll be easier to acetolyse', I continued, still swirling the vial.

'I've not done heavy liquid separation before but I can probably do the acetolysis for you', he offered.

'That would make life easier', I said with relief. It would be a large sample even after the heavy and large particles were removed and would need to be processed in several tubes. Also, if Steel did it by himself he could process it in the laboratory near our office. I would acetolyse the wattle flower samples in the laboratory I used in Earth Sciences—then there would be no question of the vacuum filter sample being contaminated by fresh wattle pollen. Good thinking.

'Why don't you come and watch me do the sieving and heavy liquid separation?' I suggested.

'That'd be great', he said enthusiastically. 'I think I'm going to learn a lot from this. But when are going to do it?' he asked.

'Thursday. I've got the darkroom booked for tomorrow and Wednesday', I said, remembering the mountain of pollen photos I had yet to print for my thesis.

'I won't be here', Steel said disappointedly. 'I'm going into the field on Wednesday and won't be back until Monday.'

'Never mind, I'll show you how to do it another time. So what have you got in that bag of goodies?' I asked, indicating the plastic bag in his open briefcase that I suspected contained the samples he'd brought in for me.

Steel reached into the bag and took out four plastic specimen jars, each containing a couple of wattle flowers. He held them so I could see the labels.

'These three are from the crime scene', he said. 'This one is labelled *Acacia* species B at the top of the label and *Acacia sophorae* at the bottom, and these two jars contain *Acacia* A and C but they're both *Acacia saligna*', he explained.

'Why are the *saligna* ones in two jars and labelled A and C?' I asked.

'That's the way the plant samples were labelled when the police gave them to me', he explained. 'They thought they were different species but the botanist at the herbarium identified them both as being *Acacia saligna*.'

'So you took these flowers off the original plant samples that the police collected from the Noosa crime scene?' I asked as I took the jars from him. I needed to make sure I understood where everything Steel was giving me came from.

'Yep, that's right', he confirmed as he held up the fourth jar, 'and this one contains the flower found inside the victim's car.'

I shuddered. Steel was handing me something that might help to prove or disprove someone guilty of murder. As I took the jar from him my shoulders drooped involuntarily with the gravity of what I had agreed to take on.

Steel delved into the bag again and took out a small cardboard box. 'Here are the tape-lift slides from the suspect's shirt and jeans that have wattle pollen on them', he said as he handed it to me. The box contained six glass microscope slides each with a portion of a tape-lift secured to one side, adhesive side up. Several of the slides were stuck together. Aghast at the possibility of losing the wattle pollen grains when the slides were pulled apart, and that such a loss could prejudice the case, I asked, 'Why didn't you put the slides in a slotted slide box so they couldn't touch each other?'

'Didn't think of that', he mumbled.

I shook my head and let the matter drop. Anyone can make a mistake. As I took the box from him, Steel's shoulders lifted as far as mine had drooped. By handing the samples to me he was absolving himself of responsibility for them. In my possession now were the samples listed in Table 5.

Table 5. Control and forensic samples Steel gave me

Forensic samples	**Control samples**
Tape-lift slides from • the suspect's jeans • the suspect's shirt. Wattle flower from inside the victim's car. Vacuum filter sample from the front driver's side of the victim's car.	Flowers from the crime scene • *Acacia sophorae* • *Acacia saligna*.

That night I sat down at my microscope to examine the samples Steel had given me. I had to determine if the pollen from the two wattle species at Noosa could be separately identified, and if the flower from the victim's car was from one of those species. First, I separated the tape-lift slides and put them in a slotted slide box. They could wait until later. The control flower specimens from the Noosa bushland were my first priority.

With fine forceps I took several anthers from each of the control flowers, mixed them with a drop of water and put a cover slip on top. This was a temporary water-mount that would be discarded after it dried out. When I looked at the pollen down the microscope I found that both species had 16 separate cells (monads) joined to form the grain. Wattle pollen is characteristically a composite grain, whereas most pollen grains are single cells. *Acacia saligna* pollen was larger than *A. sophorae* pollen, that was clear, but...and then I saw it. Each species had different patterns on the four monads in the middle of the grains. Once the pollen was processed (acetolysed) these differences would be clear enough to measure. One of Steel's problems was solved. It was possible to distinguish between pollen from the two wattle species from Noosa.

Next, I made a water mount from the flower found in the victim's car. This was the exciting bit. Would pollen from this flower be like pollen from one of the species at the Noosa crime scene, or would it be totally different? Holding my breath I plunged towards the microscope, looked down it, and focussed on the grains in the slide. Holy heck. They looked like *Acacia sophorae*.

Going back and forth between a slide of the control *Acacia sophorae* pollen and the one from the flower in the victim's car confirmed my identification. It was *A. sophorae*. This species didn't occur in Gympie and Samantha Hall's family believed that she hadn't driven her car to Noosa in the months prior to her death. But the presence of an *A. sophorae* flower in her car indicated that her car had been near *A. sophorae* plants—plants that grew where her body had been found in Noosa and that were flowering prolifically at that time. The police suspected that Samantha's own car had been used to transport her body to Noosa after she had been murdered in her home at Gympie. This piece of evidence might prove them right. It was late and there was nobody to tell except the dog. If only he could talk.

Cosby, our faithful kelpie cross, listened earnestly. My excitement was catching—he mistook 'talk' for 'walk'. Walking the dog was the last thing on my mind but walk I did, pacing up and down the house with Cosby at my heels.

The excitement walked out of me and a celebratory glass of wine in hand, I went back to my home office to look at the tape-lift slides. Having confirmed that the flower in the victim's car was the same species as one of those growing at Noosa, I now needed to see whether the pollen grains on the tape-lifts from the suspect's clothing matched either of the species from Noosa. However, the tape-lift slides were covered in fibres, soil and debris—they were a nightmare. After 10 minutes I gave up. It would take a day to find all the wattle grains. I would ask Steel to relocate them on the microscope at Scientific Section and draw a circle on the tape around the area where each grain was located. He had noted the numbered coordinates of their location on the slides in that microscope and should find them again quite quickly. The microscope Steel used was a different brand to mine and our coordinates didn't agree. His coordinates could be mathematically converted to those on my microscope, but circling the grains would be easier.

Microscope slides sit in a holder on the microscope stage, a flat platform under the objective lenses. Two small wheels (travellers) are used to move the slide back and forth (North–South) and sideways (East–West) across the stage. Along one N–S side and one E–W side of the stage are numbered centimetre scales with millimetre divisions. As the slide is moved on the stage another scale moves with it and alongside the centimetre scales on the stage. The moving scale is 0.9 centimetres long and has 10 divisions. The coordinate of a point on the slide is measured in tenths of millimetres and is found where one of the millimetre marks is level with one of the small dividing lines on the sliding scale. If we record both the N–S and E–W coordinates of a particular pollen grain on a slide, we can relocate it by re-setting the microscope to those coordinates.

The millimetre divisions along the sides of the stage also help us to methodically examined the contents of a slide, or scan the slide, as we call it, so that time isn't wasted accidentally scanning the same part of the slide twice. We start at one side of the slide, record the position from the scales on the side of the stage, then scan right across the slide to the other side. This is called a traverse. Then we go back to where we started and move the slide down or up a set number of millimetres, or parts of a millimetre, to begin another traverse directly above or below the last one.

The next morning I phoned Steel to tell him that the pollen grains from *Acacia sophorae* and *A. saligna* were different and that the flower from the victim's car had pollen comparable with that of *A. sophorae*. His response was vintage Sammy—excited and flapping. The police would be happy and off his back, and his early work on the case had not been in vain.

We arranged to meet the following Tuesday when Steel returned from his field trip. I would have sieved and done the heavy liquid separation on the vacuum filter sample by then and I could return it to him to do the acetolysis. I would also give him back the tape-lift slides to relocate the eight wattle pollen grains he had found on them—six from the suspect's shirt and two from his jeans. Not many, but it was a significant number considering the clothing had been washed on the Saturday the victim's body had been found and police had taken them from the washing line that night.

When we met on the Tuesday Steel asked me what I planned to do with the tape-lift slides after he'd circled the wattle pollen on them.

'I'll look at them under the microscope first to see if they look anything like the pollen from the Noosa species', I said slowly, trying to decide in which order I should do everything else. 'Then…I'll cut out the tape where each grain is, probably a half centimetre square bit, so that it'll fit onto the SEM stub.' (A stub is a small metal button on which samples to be viewed in scanning electron microscopes are secured.)

I continued: 'But first I'll have to find a way to process the grains to remove the lipids and cytoplasm while they're on the tape, otherwise I can't do SEM on them or get clear photos of them in the light microscope'.

'Why do you want to keep them on the tape?' Steel questioned. He had tried several ways of removing them from the tape to see them better.

'There's less chance of losing them that way', I explained, thinking about how careful we had to be with this precious evidence. 'You know, it would probably be wise to photograph them unprocessed on the tape first. At least then if any of them go missing when I process the tape we'll have a record of them.'

'I could cut out the sections of tape for you if you like', Steel offered.

I thought about this for a while. It would certainly save me time. I could still photograph them on the small bits of tape.

'Okay. That'd be great', I agreed. 'I've got another job for you as well. Can you collect two pollen samples each of *Acacia saligna* and *A. sophorae* from the herbarium?'

'Yes, I can do that, but why do want them?' he asked.

'I need to see how much their pollen varies from one bush to another and make sure that the pollen we have from the Noosa samples is representative of those species', I explained.

'That's a good idea', Steel agreed. 'The flower in the car and the pollen on his clothes could have come from different bushes.'

'Yep, that's right. There are usually only small differences in size between pollen from different plants of the same species, but we need to check that anyway', I noted.

I jotted down the things Steel was to do on a memo pad:

1. Acetolyse vacuum filter sample.
2. Cut out from the tape-lift slides the sections of tape containing wattle pollen grains.
3. Collect pollen reference samples of *Acacia saligna* and *A. sophorae* from the herbarium.

Having Steel's help would save me time. I could get on with processing the flower samples he had given me and finding a way to treat the tape sections.

The following week I acetolysed and made slides from half of the control flower samples from Noosa as well as some pollen from the flower found in the victim's car so that I could see the similarities and differences between their pollen clearly. I needed to keep the other half of the flowers in case something went wrong while I was processing the first half, and also to have some pollen to photograph unprocessed. I had to cover all angles.

While the wattle pollen samples boiled in the acetolysis mixture I experimented with ways of processing the tape-lifts. I'd cut two small sections of tape with no pollen on them from the tape slides before I'd given them back to Steel, and had drawn 'mud maps' of the debris on them. The 'maps' would serve to compare what was originally on the tape sections with what was left after my processing attempts. If one tape section was destroyed during acetolysis I could try something else with the other section.

After acetolysing the first tape section and rinsing it in acetic acid then water, I checked it in the small laboratory microscope. Not a scrap of adhesive or debris was left on it. If the tape had contained a pollen grain, that also would have been lost. It was a possible way to remove pollen from the tape—it would be in the acetolysis mixture. But trying to retrieve a single pollen grain from that would be too risky. So much for the acetolysis idea. What next?

Someone had suggested using a solution of potassium hydroxide (KOH) to remove the pollen cytoplasm and outer lipids. This alkaline solution can destroy organic matter and, over a period of time, it destroys pollen. There was nothing to lose by trying a well-diluted solution. I put the remaining tape section into 10% KOH and boiled it for ten minutes. Success—the tape adhesive and its captive debris was intact. Problem two solved.

Later that week I examined the slides I'd made of the acetolysed pollen from the wattle control samples from Noosa to describe and measure the differences between the two species, *Acacia saligna* and *A. sophorae*. Although *I* could see the differences clearly, they had to be documented for lay persons such as police and judiciary personnel.

Using the 100 μm scale in one of the microscope lenses I measured the equatorial diameter of 20 pollen grains from each species to determine their size range. On average, *Acacia saligna* pollen was 8–10 μm larger than *A. sophorae* pollen.

The patterns on the four central cells (monads) of each species were the main distinguishing features (Plate 19). On both species these central monads had thin furrows roughly following the shape of the cells and encircling a raised 'island' of the outer wall (tectum). I decided to call these areas encircled by the furrows 'tectal islands'. In *Acacia saligna* pollen, these tectal islands were irregularly divided into four or five raised areas that were not necessarily the same shape on each monad. In *Acacia sophorae* pollen most of the tectal islands on the central monads were divided into two separate 'pillows', but sometimes one or two of the islands were partially divided and occasionally one was undivided. All of these patterns could occur on the same grain.

My next task was to confirm that the acetolysed pollen from the flower found in the victim's car was identical to *Acacia sophorae* pollen. It was, except for an average size difference of 2–3 μm. Pollen from the same species may vary in size by up to 10 μm so this was negligible. Now I had one confirmed link (Table 6). Someone who had walked through an area where *Acacia sophorae* was flowering had sat in the driver's side of the victim's car.

Table 6. Evidence progress list 1

Forensic samples		**Identification (known locality)**
Wattle flower from inside victim's car	=	*Acacia sophorae* (crime scene)

Two weeks after our last meeting I met with Steel again in our office. He had with him the sections of tape containing wattle grains that he'd cut from the tape-lift slides from the suspect's clothing, and also the pollen reference samples of *Acacia sophorae* and *A. saligna* that I'd asked him to collect from the herbarium. He was excited to learn that I'd found a way to process the pollen grains on the tape sections. Both his initial 'insurmountable' problems had now been solved. Pollen from the Noosa wattle species could be separately identified, and it was possible to process the pollen grains on the tape-lifts.

Steel bent down and picked up his briefcase, put it on his desk and opened it.

'These are the pollen samples you wanted from the herbarium', he said, as he passed me four small brown envelopes from his briefcase.

'Thanks, I appreciate you doing that', I said, taking them from him. Next, he took two yellow-topped plastic specimen jars from his briefcase.

'Here are the cut-outs from the tape sections. I've put the six from his shirt in one jar and the two from his jeans in the other jar', he explained as he gave them to me.

I held them up to the light to see the sections. To my dismay, the pieces of tape were tiny, no more than 3 millimetres square, and were either stuck to each other or to the side of the jars. I took a while to find my voice, but when I did the stress of juggling my thesis and the case work came with it.

'Why didn't you use double-sided sticky tape to secure each of the tape sections onto separate glass slides, and then put them in a slotted slide box?' I said, emphasising the last two words.

'I didn't think of it', he said, looking down at the floor as he realised what the consequences might be. 'I couldn't find any slide boxes in at Scientific Section anyway.'

'Well you could have at least put them on separate slides. I'm going to have hell's own trouble getting these tiny things apart without losing the pollen grain on them', I said, my voice beginning to rise.

Sammy Steel was renowned for doing things in a rush because he was eager to please. He looked at me warily, shifting from foot to foot and fidgeting with his hands behind his back as if waiting for punishment. I weakened and let the anger seep out before I spoke again.

'All right then, I don't think carefully enough sometimes either. I'm sure some of the grains will have survived', I reassured him. His swaying movement slowed and the twisting hands emerged from behind his back.

'So what do you want me to do now?' he asked a little too quickly and eagerly. Sammy was good at changing the subject and being instantly jolly when he felt uncomfortable. I humoured him and didn't pursue the tape-section disaster. Perhaps I could have been more tactful or given him more explicit instructions.

'I've got a smaller list for you this time', I joked. 'One, get that vacuum filter sample acetolysed and two, collect pollen reference samples of the wattle species you found at Gympie from the herbarium.' Steel nodded and wrote my requests down in his diary.

At home that night I tackled the onerous task of safely removing the small tape sections and the prized wattle grains they held from their jars. Static electricity was against me. As fast as I pulled them off the side of the jar or pulled them apart, they headed back home to the side of the jar. Then disaster struck as I coaxed a stubborn tape section to relinquish its hold. Ping—out of the jar and onto the carpet. The dog was banished from the room. How stupid could I be? But then, one mistake begets another.

My knees had carpet burns by the time my minuscule friend was found—and joy, oh joy, it still carried its pollen grain. Scanning the other tape sections, now secured on their own microscope slides, was not such a happy exercise. Three of the eight tape sections didn't have a wattle pollen grain on them. The grains may have broken up or fallen off the tapes when I prised the slides apart the first time Steel had given them to me in a cardboard box, or perhaps they'd been lost when I pulled the tiny tape sections apart or from the sides of the specimen jars. Who knows. I felt ill at the thought of losing three tiny pieces of evidence—two wattle grains from the shirt tapes and one from the jeans. However, there was little I could do about it now. I would have to make the best of the five pollen grains left on the tape sections.

Now for the best part. Identifying the pollen grains. The dog was back in my office and sleeping at my feet as usual. If what I found was exciting, we could again share the moment.

Making water mounts for the tape sections proved difficult. The tape sides were curled and the cover slip had to be held down to flatten them. My other hand did everything else—focus, move the slide and change magnifications. Normally, one hand would be on the focus wheel and one on the traveller wheel.

At x 200 magnification, the four grains from the suspect's shirt appeared to be similar in size to pollen of *Acacia sophorae*, the same Noosa species the flower in the victim's car was from. The remaining grain, from the suspect's jeans, was much smaller. When I looked at all of the grains at x 1000 magnification I could see their surface ornamentation quite well. The small grain was pitted or dimpled all over and had no tectal 'islands' on the central monads like the species from Noosa did. I called this *A.* sp. 'dimpled'. (Plate 20 illustrates pollen from the tape-lifts photographed in water mounts.) The next grain I looked at was similar to *A. sophorae* but the tectal islands were smaller and almost round, and none of the tectal islands on its central monads was divided. On some of the *A. sophorae* grains I had seen, one of the central monads had an undivided tectal island but none had undivided tectal islands on all four of the central monads. Could this pollen grain be from a different species or was it a variation of *A. sophorae* pollen? I noted it down as '?*A. sophorae*'.

The presence on the tape-lifts of one, or possibly two, wattle pollen grains from species other than those known from the crime scene posed a host of questions. Were they from one of the Gympie species? Were other wattle species growing near the crime scene at Noosa?

Hoping the remaining three tape sections held answers, not more questions, I prepared their water mounts and peered hopefully at them down the microscope. Bingo. Three perfect examples of *Acacia sophorae* pollen—all from the suspect's shirt. The suspect alleged that he hadn't been to Noosa for quite some time and hadn't driven the victim's car. Furthermore, the only wattle plants that he had allegedly been near were those in Gympie. So how did three *A. sophorae* pollen grains get on his shirt? Perhaps, as the police suspected, he had driven the victim's car?

It was another 'Holy heck' moment. Cosby raised one tired eyebrow to see what the excitement was about, closed it, sighed, and went back to sleep. He had already been for a walk.

The Bricks

It was now exactly three weeks since I'd agreed to work on Samantha Hall's case. So far I had identified the flower in the victim's car and at least three pollen grains on the suspect's clothing as being from *Acacia sophorae*. This connected the car and the suspect to an area where *A. sophorae* grew. I could now add these results to my progress list (Table 7).

Table 7. Evidence progress list 2

Forensic samples		Identification (known locality)
Wattle flower from inside victim's car	=	*Acacia sophorae* (crime scene)
Pollen on tape sections from suspect's shirt	=	3 *Acacia sophorae* (crime scene) 1 ?*Acacia sophorae*
Pollen on tape section from suspect's jeans	=	*Acacia* sp. 'dimpled'

Methodically I thought through what else I knew about *Acacia sophorae*. Because of its preferred habitat—coastal dunes—it was not known to grow in Gympie and it definitely didn't occur in the areas of Gympie that the victim and suspect frequented. It didn't occur naturally in Noosa and nearby areas. It had been abundantly planted in Noosa Woods to stabilise the man-made sand spit built to extend Noosa Woods in 1978. Since then *A. sophorae* had proliferated in the bushland adjacent to the car parks in this parkland. It was here that Samantha Hall's body had been found—among flowering *A. sophorae* bushes.

Impartiality aside, it was difficult to believe that the occurrence of an *Acacia sophorae* flower in the victim's car and its pollen on the suspect's clothing was a coincidence, or that their presence had nothing to do with the site where the victim's body was found. On the contrary, the police could probably use this evidence to arrest the suspect. However, these two pieces of evidence were separate bricks in the wall of evidence. If the pollen evidence were to be used in court I would prefer that the suspect could be more firmly associated with the victim's car.

The vacuum filter sample from the victim's car was yet to be examined. Could it confirm the link between the car and the suspect? Steel still hadn't acetolysed this sample. While waiting for him to do so I would consolidate the evidence already in hand.

When I had begun to work on the case it had seemed so simple. Now it was getting complicated. Everything had to be cross-referenced, documented and verified. In a sense, Steel had been right. To show that pollen from the control plant samples from Noosa was similar to, or different from, pollen from the forensic samples (the vacuum filter sample, tape-lifts and the flower from the car), the control and forensic pollen had to be in the same state. That is, either both had to be processed to remove the pollen goo (e.g. acetolysed or treated with KOH) or they had to remain unprocessed. In truth, both of these methods had to be used.

The pollen samples had to be compared unprocessed in case, for example, some of the grains on the tape sections were lost while they were being processed. But it was from processed pollen samples that the similarities and differences between them could be seen more clearly to confirm their identification, and from which light and SEM photography could be used to illustrate this for lay persons. For this reason all the control and forensic pollen samples had to be photographed both unprocessed and processed.

What had yet to be done was buzzing around in my head in no particular order. I decided to make a list of things To Be Done, a TBD list, and prioritise it. To give myself a little instant gratification, I included those things that had already been completed, and then ticked them off (Table 8, page 128).

Table 8. Plan of action for case work (To Be Done list)

SAMPLE	TBD: M = me, S = Steel	Done?
A. Vacuum filter sample from driver's side of car	1. Sieve and heavy liquid separation. [M]	✓
	2. Acetolyse half of sample. [S]	
	3. Make slides. [M]	
	4. Look for wattle pollen in the sample and identify. [M]	
	5. Photograph pollen found in sample both before and after processing. [M]	
B. Tape-lift slides from suspect's clothing	1. Relocate wattle grains on slides and cut out tape section they are on. [S]	✓
	2. Look at wattle grains on tape sections and identify. [M]	✓
	3. Find some way to treat tape to remove pollen goo. [M]	✓
	4. Photograph unprocessed. [M]	
	5. Treat tape sections with wattle grains on them. [M]	
	6. Confirm ID of pollen on treated tapes and photograph. [M]	
	7. Do SEM. [M]	
C. *A. sophorae* and *A. saligna* pollen from Noosa	1. See if they are structurally different. [M]	✓
	2. Process (acetolyse) half of samples and make slides. [M]	✓
	3. Describe pollen morphology. [M]	✓
	4. Photograph unprocessed and processed. [M]	
	5. Prepare for and do SEM. [M]	
D. Flower from car	1. Compare unprocessed pollen with unprocessed Noosa pollen. [M]	✓
	2. Process half of sample and make slides. [M]	✓
	3. Photograph unprocessed and processed. [M]	
	4. Prepare for and do SEM. [M]	
E. Reference pollen from herbarium	1. Collect samples of *A. sophorae* and *A. saligna* from the herbarium. [S]	✓
	2. Process the above samples. [M or S]	
	3. Compare reference *sophorae* and *saligna* pollen with control pollen from Noosa plant samples. [M]	
	4. Collect samples of Gympie wattle species from the herbarium. [S]	
	5. Process the above samples. [M or S]	
	6. Describe and photograph Gympie pollen. [M]	
	7. Compare Noosa and Gympie pollen with pollen on tapes and in vacuum filter. [M]	

Making the list did help order my thoughts, but it did nothing for my stress levels. There was more to do than I'd thought and when it was done there was a statement to write. My thesis work was getting further and further behind. I decided to set aside two days a week to work on the case and spend the rest of my time on my thesis. This meant that the case work might be finished in about a month.

It wasn't possible to fast-track the case work because things like the microscope camera, SEM machine, photography darkroom and palynology laboratory had to be booked well in advance. In particular, the SEM machine could only be booked by each user for four hours a week. I'd booked a two-hour session on the Friday of the next week and two sessions in each of the following two weeks, but the light microscope photography had to be done first.

Later that week I cajoled and pleaded with one of my Earth Sciences supervisors to let me take the microscope camera home for the weekend. It wasn't meant to leave campus but the rules were often bent because of my family commitments. I was in luck—and after our usual exchange of jovial bantering he granted my wish.

Over the weekend I photographed unprocessed and processed pollen grains from the *Acacia sophorae* and *A. saligna* control samples from Noosa and from the flower found in the victim's car, and the unprocessed wattle grains on the tape-lift sections. The latter proved as troublesome as I had expected. While my left hand pressed down on the coverslip to flatten the tape section under it, my right hand had yet another job to do—press the button on the camera.

On the Monday I tracked down Steel to find out if he had acetolysed the vacuum filter sample and collected pollen of the Gympie species from the herbarium. He'd done neither and didn't think he could find time to work on them until the end of the next week. He seemed withdrawn and not as keen to help and be a part of the process as he had been in the beginning. Something was bothering him.

'I can't do much more until you acetolyse the vacuum filter sample and collect the Gympie pollen. Surely you can find an hour or so to at least do the vacuum filter sample sooner than late next week?' I asked.

A stubborn Taurus look came over his face and I could sense his foot about to paw the ground. 'Why is it so urgent?' he asked.

'Apart from the police agitating for a result I've found three definite *Acacia sophorae* grains on the tape sections, one probable *sophorae* and a small grain that's dimpled all over and nothing like *sophorae*', I explained.

Steel was startled. He'd forgotten about the tape sections.

'Yes!' he exclaimed, punching his fist in the air. 'We've got him!'

I smiled, enjoying his enthusiasm and change of mood. 'Not so fast. We still can't place the suspect in the car—well, not to my satisfaction anyway.'

'That's why you want the vacuum filter sample soon?' he asked.

'Yes—and I need the Gympie pollen to compare with the dimpled wattle grain on the clothing tape', I explained.

Steel sighed. 'OK, I'll get the vacuum filter sample to you later this week or early next week—but when are you doing SEM on the *sophorae* and *saligna* pollen samples from Noosa and pollen from the flower?' he asked, animated once again.

'On Friday', I replied. 'Tomorrow I'm preparing them for SEM and I'll also process one of the tape-lift sections. You're welcome to come and watch me in the lab and on the SEM', I offered.

At last I would be doing SEM on the tapes, as he had promised police. Enthusiastically he arranged to meet me on Friday outside the Centre for Microscopy and Microanalysis (CMM).

The next morning I dropped into our office to check on the 'goss' and leave Steel a note. I would be in the Earth Sciences laboratory for the next two hours.

For the SEM microscope I used at that time the samples had to be completely dry. If they had water in them it was almost impossible to get a good image and it could damage the microscope. To dry pollen samples they are taken through an alcohol dehydration series. Alcohol evaporates much faster than water and a small drop of pollen residue in alcohol dries out in no time. The dehydration series gradually replaces the water in the sample with alcohol so as not to damage the sample by changing the liquid it's suspended in too quickly.

The first step in the dehydration series would be to put each sample into a 25% ethanol (alcohol)–75% water solution in a small centrifuge tube, mix it well, centrifuge it, and tip off the supernatant (ethanol–water solution). I would then do the same first with 50% and then with 75% ethanol–water. After two rinses in 100% ethanol I would transfer the sample from the centrifuge tube to a small storage vial that I could take home to prepare the SEM stubs.

While the tubes spun in the centrifuge for their first ethanol–water rinse I prepared the 10% KOH solution in which to boil a tape section containing an *Acacia sophorae* grain. I was being cautious, working on one at a time. If this grain were lost there were two other tape sections with *A. sophorae* grains on them.

The tape section and the pollen grain on it survived the KOH treatment. It was over the first hurdle. As a matter of routine I sequentially soaked it in the ethanol–water solutions to dehydrate it. What should have been a similarly routine microscope check after it had been dehydrated turned into a long and frantic search. The adhesive had turned to a jelly that engulfed everything on the tape, and somewhere among the tangle of jelly-coated fibres was a precious pollen grain. No amount of prodding with a dissecting needle convinced this jelly mass to give up its hostage. I had stuffed up big time by not testing the effect of ethanol on the tape. My heart sank to my navel. As I had said to Steel when he didn't put the tiny tape-sections containing wattle pollen from the suspect's clothing onto separate slides—I sometimes don't think carefully enough either.

How could I be so stupid? Standing in front of the microscope, leaden feet rooted to the floor and eyes focussed on them, I struggled to find a positive in this negative. Where was my philosophy now? I taught my daughters that something good always came out of something bad. Just as Maria said in their favourite movie, *The Sound of Music*, 'when a door closes, somewhere a window opens'. The only positives I could find were that only one pollen grain had been lost, not five, and that the now lost pollen grain had been photographed.

Steel knocked on the laboratory door as the tubes containing the reference pollen samples went into the centrifuge for their last ethanol rinse. Together we finished the pollen dehydration series and I showed him how to pipette the residues into their storage vials without losing any pollen that might stick to the sides of the pipette and the centrifuge tube. We spoke of the pollen grain I had just lost on the tape section and those that went missing from three other tape sections, and I sensed that he was relieved that I too made mistakes. For us both this case work was a matter of trial and error. It was a learning experience and we would be much the wiser for it in future.

That night I prepared the SEM stubs by taking a small amount of the pollen residue and ethanol from each vial with a micropipette (very fine glass tube) and dropping it onto a small circular glass cover slip. When the pollen dried the cover slip was secured to an SEM stub with a sticky dot. An SEM stub is a circular metal disc about 1.25 centimetres in diameter with a small metal rod projecting from its base. This rod slots into a hole in the stub holder that goes into the SEM. Before going into this large microscope the specimen and stub surface is coated with a fine film of carbon, gold or platinum that will deflect most of the electrons from the surface of the specimen.

We began the Friday SEM session with a tour of the Centre for Microscopic Analysis (CMM). Steel hadn't been there before and was fascinated by the size and variety of electron microscopes designed for different types of analyses. Much like cars, there are the 'Rolls Royce' varieties and the everyday ones. The SEM I used at that time was multitalented. It could analyse the minerals in rocks and also reveal the surface features of biological specimens and other solid materials. Spiders, bees, ants and other small animals and plant particles were put into the SEM whole—dead, of course—whereas for larger animals and plants small sections of interest were cut to fit a stub. A large gum leaf wouldn't fit, but a small section of it would. Pollen is at the other end of the size spectrum. Thousands of grains can fit onto a stub.

To earn a licence to drive an electron microscope one has to learn the rudiments of how they work. In my first electron microscopy course we had two days of physics and two days to play with the microscopes. I'm no whiz at physics and my husband predicted that I would come home none the wiser. This made me determined to prove him wrong, and to my surprise I now have a basic understanding of how SEMs work.

In simple terms, an electron gun emits electrons from a heated tungsten filament and shoots them down the microscope column to bombard the surface of the specimen. Because electrons will be deflected by anything they hit (including air particles and dust), the column operates under high vacuum and at a chilly temperature (to reduce movement of any particles) maintained by liquid nitrogen. The electrons are focussed towards the specimen by magnetic fields produced by electromagnetic lenses situated along the side of the column. Upon hitting the specimen surface some electrons are absorbed, but most are deflected by the conductive coating on the specimen (i.e. gold, carbon). The angle at which they are deflected depends on the topography of the part of the specimen they hit. A detector reproduces this deflection as a digital or video image on a screen. The microscope operator twiddles various dials or punches keys on the keyboard to adjust the focus, magnification and other variables until the picture is as good as it can be—then presses the 'take photo' button.

The SEM we used was quite new and, unlike the old one I had learnt on five years previously, it was computerised. This 'Rolls Royce' SEM was capable of magnifying samples up to 500 000 times their normal size. Like all microscopes in the CMM it had its own air-conditioned room—warm clothing was a must even in summer. In winter, quick trips to the tea room to thaw out frozen fingers were not unusual. Science can be painful.

The first stub we put into the microscope was labelled '*Acacia sophorae* control'. Steel sat beside me, eagerly waiting for an image of pollen to pop up on the video screen—immediately. He jiggled and squirmed impatiently for ten minutes while air was evacuated from the specimen chamber and the microscope settings were adjusted for imaging pollen. The only light in the room came from the video screen and keyboard. When the microscope emitted a loud whooshing sound Steel evacuated his chair and headed for the door. Laughing,

I explained that the whoosh signalled that the chamber was under vacuum and we could now push the stub into the column and begin imaging the pollen.

Starting at a low magnification we searched for a good grain, then racked up the magnification dial to x 5000 to zoom in on the tectal islands on the central monads. Wow. Every pollen grain viewed in SEM deserves a 'wow'. The intricacies of their surface sculpture are fascinating and *Acacia sophorae* and *A. saligna* pollen didn't disappoint us. The resulting photographs clearly showed the differences between the two species (Plate 19).

At the end of our SEM session Steel gave me the acetolysed vacuum filter sample. He was again enthusiastic about being involved in the case work and had found time to work on the sample since we'd met earlier in the week. Later that afternoon I made six permanent microscope slides from the residue by using only a very small drop of it mixed in a plastic mounting medium. I took the slides home to dry over the weekend and planned to analyse them early the next week. We had arranged to meet with police to discuss our progress the following Thursday and there was no rush to analyse the slides. I needed a Saturday off. Sunday morning I would be back in the CMM at 6.00 am slicing up coal in order to pay the bills, and on Monday my mother would be arriving from Perth for her annual two-week visit. Oh joy. I needed some mothering.

The six slides from the vacuum filter sample yielded gold—12 golden wattle pollen grains. Considering that only a tiny portion of the vacuum filter residue had been used to make the slides, finding 12 wattle grains in them was significant. There would be hundreds, even thousands more in the sample if it was all made into slides and examined. Of the 12 wattle grains, nine were *Acacia sophorae* pollen and three were like the small dimpled wattle pollen grain found on the tape section from the suspect's jeans. This was it. The extra evidence we needed. My evidence progress list was growing (Table 9, page 134).

The presence of *Acacia sophorae* pollen and the unidentified dimpled wattle pollen both on the suspect's clothing and in the victim's car—in similar proportions—provided a compelling link between the suspect and the car. It was another 'Holy heck' moment. Now there were three adjoining bricks of evidence: the wattle flower in the car, the two types of wattle pollen in the car vacuumings, and the same two wattle species on the suspect's clothing. Could this be enough to arrest the suspect and convict him? Not so fast, Sherlock: if it goes to court you still have to convince others that the wattle pollen couldn't have arrived on the clothing and in the car by chance.

Table 9. Evidence progress list 3		
Forensic samples		**Identification (known locality)**
Wattle flower from inside victim's car	=	*Acacia sophorae* (crime scene)
Pollen on tape sections from suspect's shirt	=	3 *Acacia sophorae* (crime scene) 1 ?*Acacia sophorae*
Pollen on tape section from suspect's jeans	=	*Acacia* sp. 'dimpled'
Pollen in vacuum filter from front driver's side of victim's car	=	*Acacia sophorae* (crime scene) *Acacia* sp. 'dimpled'

To me, the pollen evidence was solid. But a lay person would still ask: 'Couldn't it have blown into the car and onto the clothes on a really windy and rainy day?' I would have to explain about the different ways pollen is transported.

There were several grains of wind-borne pollen, from pine trees and grasses, in the vacuum filter sample from the victim's car and on the clothing tape-lifts. But the heavier insect-transported wattle pollen was present in greater numbers than all of the wind-transported pollen types together. Wattle pollen grains are only very rarely carried by strong winds, so their high numbers relative to the wind-pollinated pollen present in the vacuum filter sample meant that they had to have been carried into the driver's side of the car on the clothing of the driver. Furthermore, for some wattle pollen to remain on the suspect's shirt and jeans after they had been washed, there must have been a large amount of pollen on them before they were washed. The wearer could only have collected large numbers of wattle pollen on his clothing by brushing against flowering plants.

The rain question was simple to answer. Plants, like animals, don't waste their male sex cells in unfavourable conditions. They wait until the atmosphere is right to go about their mating business. The anthers of insect-pollinated flowers need warmth to dehisce (split) and expose their pollen grains for the pollinators to collect. This usually happens in the morning. If it rains in the morning after several hours of sunshine a few wattle pollen grains might be carried a short distance by rain. However, this would also be true for wind-pollinated plants at the same location. Again, the amount of wattle pollen present on the clothing tapes and in the vacuum filter relative to the wind-transported pollen ruled out the possibility that all of it could have been transported into the car or onto the suspect's clothing by rain.

This technical reasoning aside, if the *Acacia sophorae* pollen did arrive on the clothing or in the car by wind and rain, the clothing and car must have been close to flowering *A. sophorae* plants. It came back to the same conclusion—that the relatively high occurrence of *A. sophorae* grains in the car and on the clothing showed that, no matter how they arrived there, the car and clothing had been near *A. sophorae* plants.

Satisfied that I could show a strong connection between the suspect, the victim's car and the Noosa crime scene, I tackled the next problem: the dimpled pollen grains in the vacuum filter and on the clothing tape-lift. Were they from the same species? The pollen grain on the tape hadn't been processed, so its surface dimples were not as prominent as those on the dimpled pollen in the processed vacuum filter. To confirm that they were the same species the tape section would have to be processed and its pollen examined in more detail.

We met Detective Inspector Alan Bourke, who was now in charge of the case, for lunch on Thursday at the trendy Wordsmiths Café. This leafy venue with green director's chairs and umbrellas above the outdoor tables is attached to the University of Queensland's bookshop. It was our office group's favourite non-alcoholic watering and feeding hole.

We ate and made small talk before getting down to business. Thus far, Alan only knew that the flower found in the victim's car had been identified as coming from *Acacia sophorae*. After briefly reporting that *A. sophorae* pollen also occurred on the tape-lifts from the suspect's clothing and in the vacuum filter sample, I began a summary of what still had to be done. Part way through explaining that the dimpled grain on the tape section had to be processed, photographed and have SEM done on it to compare it with similar grains in the vacuum filter sample, Alan sat forward in his chair and interrupted me.

'Then we can pick him up tomorrow', he said animatedly.

'You can?' I asked, my voice rising in disbelief.

'Yes. We've had the "dogs" down south onto him for the last six months so we know where he is', he explained.

An image of a man being savaged by dogs on a monthly basis sprang to mind. Surely not.

'Dogs? What are the dogs?' I asked Alan.

'The surveillance guys', he said, a little surprised at my ignorance. 'They've been watching him for us.'

I had just learnt the first word in my 'police speak' vocabulary. Steel smiled knowingly. He had friends and family in the police service and was familiar with the term.

'You mean that the pollen evidence so far is enough to arrest the suspect?' I queried. 'Yes, it's plenty', Alan explained.

Sammy and I exchanged looks. We were both delighted that our work had produced a good enough result to help arrest the suspect. But I still had misgivings about using the evidence as it stood. I wasn't entirely certain yet that the dimpled pollen grain on the tape section was the same as those in the vacuum filter sample, thus more firmly linking the suspect to the victim's car. I put this to Alan.

'Could you wait a couple of days before arresting him?' I asked. 'I'd like to confirm that the dimpled grain on the tape is the same as those in the vacuum filter', I explained.

Steel nodded in agreement and together we explained the importance of this solitary grain. The presence of pollen from the same *two* wattle species in similar proportions in the front driver's side of the victim's car and on the suspect's clothing, and with few other pollen types present, provided a compelling link between the suspect and the car. It showed contact had taken place between the clothing and the driver's side of the car.

'OK', he agreed. 'If you're worrying about the strength of your evidence we have another wattle flower that was found on the rear numberplate of the victim's car—I'll get that to you as soon as possible', Alan offered.

'That'd be great', I replied, surprised that there was an exhibit we hadn't been given. 'Do you need me to look at the Gympie wattle pollen before you arrest him?'

'No, but you'll need to examine them before writing your statement', he explained.

'How long before we have to prepare statements?' I asked.

'Oh, a few weeks yet; we'll let you know. Just concentrate on the pollen grain on the tape for now. You'll have the results of that by the weekend', he stated. It wasn't a question.

'Should have. I can process the tape this afternoon and the SEM is booked for tomorrow evening.' That was a stroke of luck; bookings had to be made a week in advance.

'I'll phone you first thing the next morning to get the results—that's Saturday', he confirmed as he stood and shook hands with us.

Steel and I stood still, outwardly calm and collected as Alan Bourke walked to his car. As he disappeared from our line of sight we turned to each other, huge grins spreading across our faces as we erupted into a 'Yes!' and a victory jig. Our battle through the maze of forensic exhibits and control samples, and the obstacles they posed, had been worthwhile. For me, there was still work to be done before Saturday and Alan's phone call, but over the weekend I would free to enjoy time with my mother and help my friend Miira with her garage sale.

The Mortar

The garage sale was advertised to begin at 8.00 am on Saturday. The remnants of sleep were still in my eyes when our first customers arrived at 6.30 am—dealers, of course. We had expected that, and sent them away. There's nothing worse than unpacking boxes while dealers rummage through them. We rolled our eyes at each other as they left. There was no need to speak.

Our joint adventures had begun over 30 years ago. First at high school, then teachers college, overseas and more recently in Brisbane for three years. Miira had gone back to Perth late the year before, not sure whether she would stay. But she did stay and had come back to Brisbane to sort out belongings she had left in the garage of her rented house. She was staying with me, as was my mother, and it was like old times. Mum was at home cooking and looking after the children; for a couple of days Miira and I had no family responsibilities.

After my successful SEM session the night before we had worked until 1.00 am preparing for the garage sale. Both dazed and still half asleep, we sat down for a wake-me-up cup of tea and to review the prices on the goods for sale. My mobile phone rang as we sat down. It was Detective 'Somebody' wanting to know the results of my SEM session.

'Yes. I'm happy with the evidence now', I told him.

'Good, thanks', and he rang off.

By 7.30 am we had three non-dealer customers. The mobile rang again. It was Detective 'Somebody' number two with the same question, and he wanted to know more than a yes or a no. Not wanting to discuss this in front of customers I braved the jungle in the corner of the backyard and its resident wildlife before continuing the conversation.

'Yes, it's the same. No, I don't need to do any more work on it...' And so it went.

At 8.30 am it happened again, and it was back to the corner jungle and carpet snakes.

'Hi Alan, no it's not too early to call me. Those mates you gave my phone number to started calling me two hours ago...So yours will be the last phone call?...Good, and good luck.' I rang off.

The bricks of pollen evidence were now connected and it was up to the police to use them.

During the couple of days that followed the garage sale, murders and forensic palynology were far from my thoughts as I helped Miira pack and spent time with my family. Returning to the girls' rooms at bedtime on the Tuesday night with the obligatory glasses of water, a TV news summary caught my eye: a man had been arrested for the murder of Samantha Hall. An image of him arriving at Brisbane airport in the company of detectives flashed across the screen. Police had arrested Reas Holden.

With my mother and Miira having returned to Perth a week after the garage sale, it was back to work as usual. Although the pollen evidence had played a major role in the arrest of Reas Holden there was still much to be done. It had to stand up to rigorous questioning in court and my statement was to be presented so that lay persons could understand the significance of the pollen evidence. *Acacia sophorae* pollen from the forensic samples had to be photographed in SEM and light microscopy to be shown beside photographs of *A. sophorae* pollen from the crime scene; pollen grains from the Gympie wattle species had to be processed, photographed and described to show that they were not like *A. sophorae* pollen grains; and whether the dimpled wattle pollen in the vacuumings and on Holden's clothing came from Gympie or somewhere else had to be investigated.

Steel had collected the Gympie pollen samples and the wattle flower from the victim's car's numberplate that Alan Bourke had promised, and we arranged to meet at the small refectory near our office building that morning. Running late for our meeting, I was worried that he'd given up on me...but he was there, mooching in the shadow of a doorway. We bought a coffee and sat down at a table in the sun outside the refectory. He seemed troubled again, as he had been several weeks beforehand when I'd asked him again to acetolyse the vacuum filter sample, but I decided not to pry into his reasons. We exchanged small talk before Steel passed me the vial containing the flower from the rear numberplate of the victim's car and the small envelopes containing Gympie wattle pollen samples he'd collected from the herbarium.

There were eight envelopes in total—two samples each from four species. Two of them, *Acacia falcata* and *A. aulacocarpa*, had been positively identified by the herbarium botanist from the plant samples Steel had collected from Gympie. The other two, *A. cowleana* and *A. holosericea*, were species the botanist had suggested for the plant sample she couldn't positively identify.

Back at my microscope later that Monday evening I took an anther from the flower found on the rear numberplate of the victim's car and made a water mount. At low magnification a clump of pollen grains came into view and I switched to a higher magnification to identify them. It was *Acacia sophorae* again. Yet another brick, or perhaps it was mortar, in the wall of evidence.

The Gympie species each proved to have different pollen. That of *Acacia falcata*, a species that grew abundantly near the victim's home, was 5–8 μm smaller than *A. sophorae* pollen and at least 15 μm smaller than that of *A. saligna*, the other species that grew near the Noosa crime scene. The monad surfaces were unlike those of *A. saligna* and *A. sophorae* and its walls were quite thin. *Acacia aulacocarpa* pollen (Plate 21A) had small, almost round, undivided tectal islands like the grain on one tape section from the suspect's clothing that I had tentatively identified as ?*A. sophorae*. Another look at the ?*A. sophorae* grain on the tape confirmed my suspicions. It was pollen of *A. aulacocarpa*, the other species positively identified at Gympie. There were three, not two, different species on the suspect's clothing. This needed some thought.

Acacia aulacocarpa flowers from February to April. The murder occurred in August, so the grain on the tape didn't come from the suspect brushing against a plant in flower at the time of the murder. The shirt had been washed before the tape-lift was taken. This pollen grain was unlikely to be the only one of its kind on the shirt before it was washed. Which part of the shirt was the tape-lift from? Ah ha! The lower front right, slightly to the side. This made sense.

Pollen is in soil near its parent plant all year round. If someone sits or kneels in that soil, or gets it on their hands and wipes it on their clothing, they transfer pollen to their clothing. If this is how the *Acacia aulacocarpa* pollen got onto the suspect's clothing, where was its parent plant? The three small shrubs of *A. aulacocarpa* that Steel found in Gympie near the areas of interest were off to the side of well-trodden pathways. The *A. aulacocarpa* pollen grain may have come from soil near these plants. Or…this species might grow in Noosa near the crime scene.

Was it possible that the police hadn't collected samples of all the wattle species at the crime scene? They're not botanists. I hadn't been to the crime scene and Steel had only seen it through the window of a police car. It was high time we went there; in hindsight, we should have visited the site before either of us took on the case. Both being novices, I excuse us. A trip to Noosa to investigate plants at the crime scene would be nice, with lunch in the cappuccino strip and a stroll around the boutiques a bonus.

Back from my reverie on the joys of Noosa, I made water mounts of pollen from the two wattle species the herbarium botanist had suggested for the one plant sample from Gympie that she couldn't positively identify. *Acacia holosericea* pollen was similar in size to that of *A. saligna* but its monads weren't furrowed. The surface of *A. cowleana* pollen was markedly dimpled (Plate 21B) and the monads were unfurrowed, but the grains were much larger than the similarly dimpled grains in the vacuum filter sample and the one on the suspect's jeans. Yet another mystery and more thinking to be done.

The dimpled pollen on the jeans and in the car vacuumings was either from an unknown wattle species, or the plant specimen from Gympie that the herbarium botanist had difficulty identifying was *Acacia cowleana* and its pollen had an unusually large size range. I leant toward the unknown species theory. But if it was from an unknown species, what was it and where did it grow? Did it grow in Gympie, Noosa or somewhere else connected with Samantha Hall's murder? Perhaps somewhere the murderer had disposed of bloodied items or another locality he had investigated as a likely place to leave her body?

A trip to Noosa was a must—and soon—to see if *Acacia aulacocarpa* and a wattle species that produced dimpled pollen grew near the crime scene. I would ask Steel to contact Paul Zohn at the Noosa CIB to arrange for us to meet him at the crime scene the following week.

Steel was waiting for me outside the Earth Sciences laboratory on the following Monday morning. It was now two months since I had begun working on the case and the end was in sight. We were to meet Paul Zohn at the Noosa crime scene on Friday. I'd acetolysed the Gympie pollen samples and the additional flower from the car the previous week. Today I would make the slides from their residues and, later, dehydrate the pollen residues from both of the flowers from the victim's car for SEM. Steel had come to watch me make the slides in a plastic mounting medium.

For decades, palaeopalynologists and modern pollen morphologists have mounted pollen in glycerine jelly and sealed the sides of the cover slips with nail varnish or similar. However, pollen tends to swell in this medium and if the varnish seal is broken and air gets into the glycerine jelly it dries out. More recently, clear plastic mediums have been used to make slides that should last 'forever'. A drop of pollen residue is mixed with a weak glue solution on a cover slip. When this dries, the cover slip is inverted and placed pollen-side down onto a microscope slide on which the liquid plastic has been smeared. The plastic hardens overnight.

We prepared three cover slips each for the Gympie pollen and left them on the hotplate to dry while we joined our office mates for morning coffee. As we walked towards Wordsmith's café, Steel and I discussed where the *Acacia aulacocarpa* grain on the suspect's shirt might have come from. We agreed that soil near a parent plant was its most likely source.

The origin of the small dimpled wattle pollen grains in the vacuum filter and on the suspect's jeans was still a mystery. The herbarium botanist had only suggested that the plant sample Steel collected from Gympie, the one she couldn't positively identify, could be *Acacia cowleana*. Steel had recently learnt that *A. cowleana* grew further inland and was not suited to growing in the Gympie area. This confirmed my suspicions that these pollen grains were from an unknown species. Might we find this unknown species at the Noosa crime scene?

The cover slips were dry when we returned. I cleaned the first three microscope slides, put the plastic mounting medium on them, and showed Steel how to invert the cover slips and place them onto the plastic mounting medium without getting air bubbles in it. I watched as he competently prepared the remainder of the slides.

The weekly meeting with my supervisors was only five minutes away and after the meeting I'd planned to dehydrate the pollen samples from the two flowers from the victim's car for SEM. But Steel was enjoying working in the laboratory and asked if he could do the dehydration while I was away. He seemed confident enough and I could see no reason to refuse his offer of help.

'If you finish the dehydration before I get back, can you pipette the pollen samples from the tubes into their vials like I showed you last time you were in here?' I asked.

'Sure, no problem', he answered. I took two glass pipettes out of the drawer. The pollen samples from the car flowers were now only small dots on the bottom of the test tubes. Some of this would be used for SEM but we needed to retain as much as possible in case some was needed at a later date, perhaps by the defence.

'Here are the pipettes', I said, placing them on a piece of paper towel on the bench. 'Make sure you rinse the sides of the tubes well and then rinse the pipette with ethanol and let it run into the vial', I instructed.

My meeting with my supervisors didn't go well. In fact it was a disaster. I came away from it angry with myself for taking on the case at all and for letting it get in the way of my thesis work. Steel had finished the dehydration series by the time I returned and was washing the tubes in the sink. As I cleaned up the laboratory benches, brusquely venting my pent-up anger on them, I noticed that something was missing.

'Where are the used pipettes?' I asked.

'Oh, I didn't use them. I've put them back in the drawer', he replied.

'How did you put the sample into the vials?' I questioned, my mood not getting any lighter.

'Just tipped them straight from the tube into the vial. I always do that', he quipped confidently.

'But that's not what I asked you to do. Did you rinse the tube sides with ethanol after you tipped the sample into the vial?' My frown was deepening.

'No, there's enough residue there anyway', he replied defensively. I sighed. There might be enough residue, but then there might not. There was nothing I could do now the tubes had been washed, but in the mood I was in I wasn't able to let this disregard of my instructions pass without comment.

'I realise you have your own way of doing things in your laboratory, but when someone else is responsible for the outcome of your actions, and gives you strict instructions, you should follow them', I said sternly. There was an uncomfortable silence. Steel left shortly afterwards without his usual cheery farewell.

...and the Roof

We were to meet Paul Zohn at Noosa CIB at 11.00 am. That gave me time to drop the girls at school, pick up Steel and get to Noosa on time—maybe. Steel was leaning against his letter box when I arrived. Solemnly he opened the back door and placed a pile of cardboard folders and newspapers on the back seat before opening the passenger door and getting in. Not a word. Things didn't look good. My firm words the previous Monday afternoon in the laboratory about following instructions had taken their toll on our friendship.

I spent the rest of the two-hour drive making inane conversation in the hope that Steel would realise there were no hard feelings on my side. I was also nervous. Aside from Alan Bourke, my only contact with police officers had involved traffic offences and random breathalysers; neither had been pleasant experiences. On the other hand, Steel knew the officers we were to meet today and had friends in the police service. This meeting held no fears for him. The tables had turned. From being boss cocky in the laboratory I now felt subordinate to Steel.

At the Noosa CIB we were ushered past the reception desk and into the office area where the real action took place. No mean traffic cops were in sight, thankfully. In an office at the end of a corridor Alan Bourke was relaxing in a chair and talking to another detective. We made small talk about the unseasonably warm weather and our drive up from Brisbane. So far so good. Paul Zohn would be here in a minute. I hoped he would be as affable and unlike my stereotypical police officer as Alan was.

Voices at the other end of the corridor alerted Steel to Paul's imminent arrival and he walked out to meet him. I followed to see Steel being greeted warmly by a tall well-built young man in plain clothes. Observing their exchanged greetings and jolly banter I revised my image of police officers to include attractive good-humoured detectives. Steel introduced us and the handshake and eye contact were confident and warm.

'So he confessed?' asked Steel.

Paul nodded in the affirmative. 'He was really quiet on the plane back from Adelaide, sleeping or probably thinking, but in the car on the way up here he opened up. We had to shut him up until we got back here and could tape a formal interview.'

This was news to me. Steel had said nothing.

'That's good news. I didn't know about that', I said, wondering why.

'Oh, Paul told me about it the other day when I phoned him. I thought you knew. Sorry', Steel apologised.

It was strange that this wasn't mentioned in the laboratory the day before. Oh well, I knew now.

'Does that mean we don't have to write a statement and go to court?' I asked with visible relief.

Paul smiled. 'Sorry, mate. You still have to do that. He won't plead guilty.'

The law and its ways were foreign to me but from what I could gather from the subsequent conversation, a confession didn't mean that the person who gave it would necessarily plead guilty. In fact it was rare for anyone to plead guilty to murder. Instead, they could allege that their confession was extracted from them under duress—and plead not guilty.

'All right, let's get going. You follow me', Paul instructed. 'We'll go down to the end of Hastings Street and continue into the park. If you're held up in traffic I'll wait for you inside the entrance to the park.'

We were held up. I was looking for a good lunch spot along Hastings Street. We caught up with Paul and followed him into the park. A short distance in, and after a few turns, we were in a car park surrounded by large trees and shrubs, and with smaller shrubs in scrubland behind them. Paul parked mid-way down the car park. We parked next to him, then followed him as he walked back towards the entrance of the car park.

This was my first crime scene and I was apprehensive. How would I feel when we came to the exact site the body had been found? It felt different already. The chic holiday town that lay metres behind us seemed kilometres away. There was an eeriness about this place, but also a warmth. I wondered about the young woman whose body lay here that August night. What she was like, her family, her friends...

My reverie came to an abrupt end as we stopped at the first parking bay on the right of the entrance to the car park.

'Here we are. This is where he allegedly backed the car in, close to these two wattle bushes. The victim was in the passenger seat, held in by the seat belt', Paul explained sombrely. The tall detective was no longer jovial, but spoke quietly and respectfully. 'We sampled this one here', he said, pointing to the bush nearest to the rear of the parking bay. 'It's that species you say the flowers in the car are from.'

That made sense. How the wattle pollen got onto Holden's clothes was now clear.

'So he would have come around the back of the car and to the passenger's side to open the door and get the victim out?' I asked. Paul nodded, and I continued: 'And as he did, he brushed against the wattle flowers and collected pollen on the back of his shirt and probably sleeves', I surmised. 'That's if he parked close to the bushes, which would make sense. They would obscure what he was doing if anyone drove into the car park.' Good thinking, Sherlock.

'Yes, that's what he alleged he did', Paul said as he led us into the bush behind the parking bay. 'Then he dragged the body through the bushes at the back of the car, down this little track and then veered off it to the left and through the scrub.' Paul walked several metres to the left.

'The body was found here, covered with branches', he said, pointing to a small weed-infested area dotted with juvenile wattle plants.

This was it. I tried to imagine the scene that night but the energy was disturbing. Must get back to business mode. This was work, not a time to become emotionally involved.

'Wonder why he put the body in an area not as densely vegetated as it is only a few metres away?' I mused.

'Oh, the scenes of crime people are responsible for the sparse vegetation. They cleared around the body looking for evidence,' Paul explained.

'So none of these small shrubs were here then?' I asked.

'Yeah, they'd be here. The guys from Scientific Section may have pulled a few out, but they would work around those a bit away from the body', he explained.

Of course. The plants were fairly well established and couldn't have grown that large since August. It was now early May the following year. Dumb question, but good news. The murderer had to brush past them, probably several times, while collecting branches to cover the body. Could one of these small plants be *Acacia aulacocarpa*, or produce dimpled pollen grains?

Standing next to the spot where the body had lain my thoughts returned to the victim. My knowledge of the case was limited to the pollen work. At this time I knew nothing of Samantha Hall and Reas Holden, what their relationship was like, what prompted this terrible crime or what other evidence the investigators had collected. As we walked with Paul back to his car I questioned him about the personal side of the case and why the investigating team chose to concentrate their efforts on Reas Holden.

Paul filled me in. Samantha Hall was the mother of two small boys, and Reas Holden was her former partner and father of her children. The relationship had been stormy at times and they had separated several months before the murder. As we spoke of this I began to realise that for police officers like Paul Zohn and Alan Bourke, working to resolve crimes that affected the lives of families and took loved ones from them was not an unemotional experience. These police officers were family people themselves. Their compassion for families affected by violent crimes and their zeal in working to solve such cases was a revelation to me—so far removed from my encounters with uniformed and dispassionate enforcers of traffic regulations.

I was also interested to know what evidence, aside from the flowers that had been found in the victim's car, supported the theory that her body was transported to Noosa in her own car. Paul related information that came from members of the public. An elderly person allegedly saw the victim's car driving along a Gympie main street about 8.00 pm on the Friday night the murder was thought to have taken place. It was driven by a man and a woman was in the front seat. This was no chance glance; the car almost knocked the person over. Then there was the truck driver who reported that at about 1.30 am on Saturday 31 August, the day the body was found, his truck almost collided with a car fitting the description of the victim's car. Heading towards Gympie on the road between Noosa and Gympie, the car was travelling fast and the driver seemed recklessly unaware of other traffic on the road.

But why were they so sure Reas Holden was driving the car? There were several reasons. They had found the keys to Samantha Hall's car in Holden's room but he couldn't explain how they got there. Witnesses reported that he'd gone into the bar of the Mt Pleasant Hotel looking for her the morning her body was found and told them she had left the keys to her car in his room. But friends and family didn't believe she would give him the keys, nor did they believe she would go to his room. Matt, Samantha's then boyfriend, was the only other person who might have driven the car—but he had a solid alibi.

Paul knew perfectly well, and statistics showed, that women were more likely to be murdered by their partner or former partner than by anyone else. Holden had presented at the Gympie police station shortly after the murder became public knowledge and had played the part of a distressed former partner well. By the end of the lengthy interview Paul conducted with him that night Paul felt that Holden's story was 'too good'. Too good to be true. It was a typical scenario.

Alan Bourke had mentioned to me and Steel that Holden had bragged about knowing how to commit the perfect murder. I was curious to know more. Was this after the murder or beforehand? It seems that when he'd been in jail, before he'd met Samantha, Holden had learnt from fellow inmates what he considered to be a foolproof method of killing someone and getting away with it. Not only had he bragged to a member of the victim's family some years beforehand that he'd learnt how to kill 'a missus', but several weeks before the murder he'd confided in an acquaintance how he would get rid of his former partner. This was not admissible in court because Holden had been drunk at the time.

Being privy to such information was a new experience for me and it served the purpose that I had hoped. I was now more comfortable with the findings of my pollen analysis.

Paul left to go back to work and Steel and I began our search for wattle species other than *Acacia sophorae* and *A. saligna*. Starting where Holden had allegedly parked the car, we walked along the path the body had been taken. I carried the cardboard folders for the plant samples and Sammy walked ahead with secateurs in his hand, bemoaning the fact that he'd left his plant identification key at home. As he pushed his way through the shoulder-high thicket of juvenile wattles he muttered, 'Same. Another *sophorae*...and...another ...another...and another'.

At that time in my life I had no interest in things botanical. I could easily recognise a flowering wattle but none of the plants at the crime scene were flowering. If I'd been asked what type of plants Steel was identifying I wouldn't have said wattle. Wattles that grew near the farm I was raised on were large trees with long thin leaves. The mature *A. sophorae* shrubs at the crime scene were much smaller and had broader leaves than my version of wattle, and the smaller plants in the thicket that Steel also identified as *A. sophorae* had different leaves again.

'How come these smaller shrubs have different leaves from the larger ones?' I asked Steel. 'Are you sure they're all *sophorae*?'

'Yes,' he replied. 'They're all the same species. The juvenile leaves are often quite different from the mature leaves.'

I could accept that. Leaves on small gum trees are often very different from those of their mature brethren, so why not wattle?

'Aren't you going to sample any of these plants?' I asked anxiously.

'I'll take a couple if you really want me to, but they're all the same', he said.

'All right, but *I* don't know they're the same. I need to be convinced. So can we collect from every small stand of trees and also from plants that are standing alone?' I asked.

Steel shrugged. 'Whatever. If that's what you want.'

We'd collected eight samples by the time we arrived at the site where the body was found. About one metre away from the site was a solitary shoulder high shrub.

'This would be a good one to collect', I commented.

'There's no point. It's exactly the same as those over there', Steel said emphatically as he pointed towards the last thicket of shrubs.

'I don't care, it looks different to me and I want a sample of it', I retorted. 'At this location it could be really important.'

Steel mumbled to himself in exasperation, cut a section off the plant, took another cardboard folder from me and with a dramatic flourish labelled it number nine. 'Where to now?' he asked.

'He could have walked back to the car park this way', I indicated. 'It's a much shorter and more direct way than going back the way he came.' Between us and the car park the trunk of a dead tree and some of its branches lay in a pile. To the right of this was an ill-defined track leading under a large tree on the edge of the car park. Even a tall man could walk under the tree at this point and not touch its foliage. It looked like my kind of wattle tree. So far the only wattles Steel had identified were *Acacia sophorae*. Was this the other wattle, *A. saligna*, that was also meant to occur at the crime scene?

'Could this one be *saligna*?' I asked Steel.

'Probably. I'll sample it if you like', he said, cooperative again.

'Let's walk around the perimeter of the car park in case he walked around to check it out before taking the body out of the car', I suggested.

There were no wattle plants at the end of the car park, but a large tree on the opposite side from the crime scene caught my eye and I stopped to admire it. The young leaves at the growing end of each small branch were a deep red. Apart from these red leaves the tree resembled my imprinted version of wattle trees. Steel disagreed with me and refused to sample it.

'It's *not* wattle, and besides, we've run out of cardboard folders', he stated.

'So? We put it between sheets of the newspaper you brought with you', I suggested.

'It's not wattle', he said adamantly, 'so we don't need to sample it.'

I had to think of another way to get him to sample it without causing more 'aggro'.

'These red tips are fascinating. Have you got any idea what genus the tree is?' Gently, gently does it.

'No, can't think offhand', he admitted. 'It's not like anything I've seen before.'

'Why don't we sample it then. It would be good to know what it is. I wouldn't mind one of these in my garden', I mused, and smiled knowingly at him with raised eyebrows in a mock query.

'OoooOh', Steel groaned with a grin. 'I give in.'

Back in Hastings Street we had lunch at an outdoor café I had spied on the way into the park. We were comfortable in each other's company again. After a wicked iced chocolate each and a stroll through a couple of tourist shops we headed back home.

The atmosphere in the car on the way back to Brisbane was of a day's work well done despite the hiccups along the way. Lunch was a treat, the weather was good and the general ambience of Noosa had rubbed off on us. Having left behind the sombreness of the crime scene we laughed and joked, our respective worries far from our minds.

Outside his home Sammy collected the folders containing the plant samples from the back seat of my car, then thanked me for a good day. I watched him as he walked up the driveway and wondered if the bridge we had just built to repair our friendship would be sustained.

The results of the herbarium botanist's identification of the plant samples we collected from Noosa were startling. Steel had, of course, been right. Most of the plant samples we collected were from *Acacia sophorae*. But on the two instances I insisted that additional samples be collected my instincts had been correct. The tree with red new growth on the other side of the car park proved to be *A. saligna*, as was the large tree near the crime scene under which I'd suggested Holden may have walked to return to the car. This explained why no *A. saligna* pollen was found in the victim's car or on Holden's clothing. The flowers were too high to be accidentally brushed against.

The plant right next to where the body had been found that Steel and I had argued about collecting, plant sample nine, proved to be *Acacia aulacocarpa*. Because *A. aulacocarpa* wasn't flowering at the time of the murder, and the three small shrubs in Gympie were in bushland off the side of a pathway, it was extremely doubtful that the *A. aulacocarpa* grain on Holden's shirt had come from them. Instead, there was a strong case for it having come from the crime scene. No doubt there were more small *A. aulacocarpa* plants at the scene at that time and small amounts of their pollen would be in soil near them, or even on their foliage. While collecting the plant material to cover the body, Holden may have uprooted small plants as well as collecting dropped branches from the surrounding vegetation. In both instances he would come in contact with soil...and wipe his hands on his clothing? The bricks and mortar were already in place and this additional evidence provided a roof. I revised my evidence progress list (Table 10).

Table 10. Evidence progress list 4

Forensic samples		Identification (known locality)
Wattle flower from inside victim's car	=	*Acacia sophorae* (crime scene)
Pollen on tape sections from suspect's shirt	=	3 *Acacia sophorae* (crime scene) 1 *Acacia aulacocarpa* (crime scene and Gympie)
Pollen on tape section from suspect's jeans	=	*Acacia* sp. 'dimpled' (?)
Pollen in vacuum filter from front driver's side of victim's car	=	*Acacia sophorae* (crime scene) *Acacia* sp. 'dimpled' (?)

Only one question remained unanswered. Where was the wattle species that produced small dimpled pollen grains? Knowing what species it came from would probably have little impact on the evidence it provided. What was important was that it occurred together with *Acacia sophorae* pollen on Holden's clothing and in the vacuum filter sample from the front driver's side of the victim's car. That these pollen types occurred in similar proportions in both the exhibits was a bonus.

The Statement

It was the end of May and all of the SEM and light microscope photography had been done (examples shown in Plate 22). My part of the investigation was finished except for my formal statement to the police. I had been dreading this, but today was the day. I was on my way to visit police headquarters in Brisbane city to discuss what was required of me. A rough copy of what I thought would be needed in the statement was sitting beside me in a folder on the passenger's seat of the car.

The directions to the visitors car park around the corner from police headquarters had been confusing. I didn't recall a side street off to the right after the lights before the Transit Centre. Yes, there it was, and at the end of the street was an entrance to a large undercover car park. There were no high gates at the entrance as had been described to me. They may have been pulled aside. I drove up to the small cubicle at the entrance and asked if this was where official visitors parked.

'No, mate', the attendant replied. 'If you back up the street a bit you'll see some high gates on your right that lead into an open car park. Pull up outside the gates and someone will let you in.'

Following these instructions I reversed and pulled into the driveway of the car park behind me and to the right, and waited. There was no one in sight. Who was going to let me in? I was already late. I got out of the car and peered through the gates and behind the high walls either side of them. Nope, no one there. Ah. There it is. A button on the wall on the right side of the gate and a small metal grille beside it like those outside high-security residential blocks. I pressed the button and waited. No one answered. Looking up at the high building beside me as I pressed the button again, I wondered if the gate was visually monitored. The grille finally came to life, asking me to state my name and what business I was on.

'I'm Lynne Milne. I've come to see Senior Sergeant Brad Hall in Scientific Section. He said he would notify you that I was coming', I said, speaking into the grille.

'That's right. Come on in', instructed the voice from the grille.

Back in my car I watched as the gates opened, hoping they would stay open long enough for me to walk back through them and onto the street to walk around to Police Headquarters. The button on the wall was out of reach from the other side of the gate if it was closed. After parking my car and gathering up the things from the seat beside me I walked briskly towards the still open gates. They began to close as I went through them. There really was someone up there watching?

I followed the directions I'd been given and found the wide bank of steps leading up to the entrance of Queensland's police headquarters. At reception I wrote and signed my name in the Visitors Book and in turn received a numbered visitors badge. Someone would be down to collect me shortly.

The row of turnstiles that ran from one side of the atriumed entrance to the other appeared to be the way in to the working part of the building. Several people came through the turnstiles but didn't head in my direction. At last a tall handsome hunk fitting my newly revised opinion of police officers was walking towards me with an outstretched hand and a welcoming smile. This might not be so bad after all. Pity they don't come a little older.

Brad Hall took me through the turnstiles with his security card and led me around to a bank of lifts. At the designated floor we went through another security door and into a wide area onto which his office opened. This was the nerve centre of Scientific Section. Further along there were laboratories and examination rooms, and a workshop below. It was much larger than I had anticipated.

As we sat down on opposite sides of Brad's desk he complimented me on the work I had done and discussed its contribution towards the arrest of Reas Holden. Before getting down to the business of my statement we discussed the sad reality of domestic conflict and violence and the terrible homicides it spawned. To emphasise a point Brad turned in his chair and reached behind him to a filing cabinet and pulled out a folder.

'Would you like to see photographs of the victim?' he asked.

'Not right now, but I may do at some other time', I replied. The mere fact that Brad thought photos of the victim would illustrate his point was enough for me. The only dead body I had seen was that of my grandmother. She had looked beautiful and restful lying in her coffin in a white satin robe. I suspected that these photos would not be so beautiful. Sensing my reticence, and possibly understanding why, Brad quietly put the folder of photographs back into the filing cabinet and we got down to the business of my statement.

The first part of the statement would list my academic qualifications, publications and work experience, to demonstrate that I was qualified to provide an expert opinion. Then a summary of the exhibits I worked on, what was done with them and the conclusions that could be drawn from them, followed by a more detailed version of what was in the summary. The latter should include dates I received exhibits or returned them, details of the procedures carried out on them, who did them and why. The scientific aspects should be written so that a lay person could understand them, and importantly, the reasons for the opinions I expressed should be clearly stated.

It was fairly straightforward. The basics of palynology accompanied by diagrams could be included, and tables of results and self-explanatory composite plates of pollen photos from the control, reference and exhibit samples would be helpful.

The only difficulty I could see ahead was that the final version of the statement was to be inserted into a special form in an Apple Mac format. I had a PC. In those days it wasn't so easy to convert from one computing system to the other, but it seemed there was someone in Scientific Section who knew how to do it.

A week later my PC version of the statement was ready to be inserted into the Mac format and I arranged to spend the day at Scientific Section finalising it. Having no trouble finding the car park this time, I walked confidently into police HQ and asked for Brad Hall. As before, we went through security and to his office. Steel was there waiting for us. It was the first time I'd seen him since our visit to Noosa some four weeks beforehand. He greeted me coolly.

Brad suggested that Steel and I go through our statements together to make sure we each had the correct dates for the exchange of exhibits between us and other things we had done together.

We went through to a laboratory where Steel had been using a Mac computer to write up his statement. Some of our dates were mixed up and we managed to sort those out, but it was another part of my statement that Steel was most interested in.

'What are you going to say about the pollen grains lost from the tape sections?' he asked defensively. He was referring to three tape sections on which, after I had prised them from the sides of the plastic vial he had put them in, I had found no wattle pollen grains.

'I've stated how many pollen grains were on the tape sections when I looked at them', I said. 'That's all I can say.'

'But I've said there were more in my statement', Steel countered.

'That's fine. You have to say it as you found it', I replied.

'But I told police how many wattle pollen grains I found when I first looked at the tapes', he insisted. 'They were on the tape sections when I gave them to you. Why can't you say there were the same number of grains on the tape sections when you got them?' he asked.

'Because when I looked at them, there weren't', I said firmly.

'Have you said how they were lost in your statement?' he asked, eyeing me suspiciously. 'No', I replied, emphasising the 'oh'.

'Who are you going to say was responsible for losing them if you're asked in court?' he challenged.

'Let's hope it doesn't come to that', I said in a conciliatory tone. 'But if it does, I'll say they were lost during transport. For heaven's sake, they could have fallen off anywhere.' Sammy put on his best surly pose and stared at me coldly. How could I reassure him that I hadn't pointed the finger at him in my statement?

'Look. I'm not going to lie', I said sternly. 'I've admitted that I accidentally lost one wattle pollen grain when I rinsed a tape section in ethanol, and I've stated how many grains there were on the tape sections when I first looked at them. That's all I can do. Here...read what I've written about it for yourself.' I shoved the statement at him and walked back to the office area to find a hot drink and a quiet corner. Sipping a cup of tea I reflected on the mishaps of the last few months. If ever I worked on another criminal case I would do it differently. There would be no middle man (as Steel had been) between me and the police; I would deal directly with the police and have some say in how pollen was collected from the forensic items; no other person would handle forensic samples I was responsible for unless I was with them; and I would think very carefully about how the samples should be handled and treated before starting work on them.

Resolved and refreshed I returned to the laboratory to find Steel more composed. The computer person had downloaded the PC version of my statement onto the Mac. The words were on the screen but the formatting had gone—paragraphs ran into each other as did many words. More drama. My computing skills had only recently taken a quantum leap from the DOS system to Windows, and playing with a mouse that didn't need feeding was still an alien concept.

The Mac computer didn't have the latest programmes on it and I floundered despite Steel's help—he, of course, had managed to do his statement on it. Again, it was my turn to be an inferior being—served me right for being bossy in the laboratory. Frustrated, I went home with the promise that the following day I could use Brad's computer, which was more up to date and easier to use.

My statement was duly completed, signed, and submitted on 3 June 1997. In summary, my expert opinions and reasons for them were:

1. The *Acacia sophorae* flowers in and on the victim's car, and the *A. sophorae* pollen in the vacuum filter sample from the front driver's side of the car, placed the car in close proximity to flowering *A. sophorae* plants.
2. *Acacia sophorae* is a coastal species and no *A. sophorae* plants were found in the areas of inland Gympie that Holden or the victim frequented.
3. *Acacia sophorae* does not occur naturally in the Noosa area, but has been abundantly planted and is proliferating in Noosa Woods/Noosa Spit, where the victim's body was found.
4. *Acacia sophorae* is insect pollinated and its heavy pollen is unlikely to be carried very far, if at all, by wind. Therefore, the flowers and pollen of *A. sophorae* were transported into the car by a person, probably on the clothing and shoes of a person who sat in the driver's seat. The fact that usually common wind-borne pollen (pine and grass) was rare in the vacuum filter sample in comparison with the amount of *Acacia* pollen in the sample further supported this opinion.
5. For *Acacia sophorae* pollen to be found in abundance in the vacuum filter sample from the front driver's side of the victim's car, the person who transported the pollen into the car must have firmly brushed against flowering *A. sophorae*.
6. The co-occurrence, in similar proportions, of *Acacia sophorae* pollen and pollen from an unknown *Acacia* species in the vacuum filter sample and on Holden's clothing suggested that he had driven the victim's car recently.

Not being familiar with how the defence counsel can pull apart an expert witness's opinion, this statement seemed fair to me at the time.

In the End

In 1997, before a case was committed to trial in Queensland it went before a district magistrate, in a pre-trial procedure called a committal. The magistrate would either commit the case to trial, decide to deal with it further in the Magistrate's Court or dismiss it. There are pros and cons for this system. One of the downsides of committals is that the defence gets two bites at the witnesses and, in the case of rape, the complainant (victim). According to one of my students who is a police officer, once a complainant in a rape case has been grilled by the defence in a committal hearing, she rarely wants to go through with a trial. She will withdraw her complaint and the charges will be dropped; if her complaint was genuine, a rapist will go free. On the positive side, committals may prevent the cost of trials when they are not warranted.

A committal is like a mini trial. Witnesses are taken through their evidence by the prosecution and questioned by the defence as they would be in a trial, but not at such length or as thoroughly. For this reason a committal may take only a couple of days or a week, whereas a trial may run into several weeks or months. For an expert witness, especially for fearful first-timers like me, a committal is a good practice run.

In September—almost three months late—my PhD thesis was finally submitted. My PhD supervisors had been benevolent regarding my tardiness up to a point, but when my thesis was one month overdue they became positively fierce, able to reduce me to tears with a mere glance of disapproval. The last two months were no fun, but the end result was worth it.

My daughters accompanied me to submit my thesis, gleefully photographing my every move: as I took the six printed copies of it, two volumes each, to be temporarily bound; as I picked up the bound volumes; as I signed and handed them over the counter of the Postgraduate Research Office; and finally, me holding the receipt to verify that I had submitted my thesis. We even asked passers by to take photos of the three us holding the twelve bound volumes. It was their day as much as mine and they delighted in my embarrassment at their antics.

I had been working on my PhD part-time over a period of eight and half years, during which I had taken one year off for illness. Belinda was just seven and Caroline three when I started; they were now 15 and 12 respectively. Neither could remember when I wasn't doing a PhD. Many requests they made during those years were answered with 'After I finish my PhD'. For us all, a new era was about to begin.

It took a month to recover and clean and clear our home of the accumulated debris from weeks of neglect. The girls had a real mum again who cooked, washed and spent time with them. This short period of normality came to an end in mid-November as we prepared to sell our home and make arrangements to move to Perth. It was a mammoth move after 12 years, especially without a man about the house to share the workload and decision making. Emotions were running high as the girls realised that the decision we made a year beforehand was coming to fruition and they would soon be leaving their friends and the town they regarded as home. Perth was where Mum came from and their Dad now lived, but aside from their father and immediate family connections, it held little for them to look forward to. It was in the midst of these preparations for the auction of our house and emotional highs and lows that the committal date fell.

I was summonsed to appear in the Magistrate's Court on the Sunshine Coast in late November 1997. Not understanding court procedures and protocol, I spoke to Brad Hall and Paul Zohn about what to expect. They were casual about it. No worries, mate—a committal was not a big deal. I was to answer the questions the prosecution and defence counsel asked me, and direct my answers to the magistrate.

On the morning of the committal southern Queensland was wet and unseasonably cold. The drive north from Brisbane took an hour and a half. Despite the weather, I arrived on time. Steel was waiting on the steps to the courthouse and I joined him. It was the first time we'd met since preparing our statements together in Scientific Section. He had moved from our office because he had changed supervisors. I expressed my pleasure at seeing him, and he responded in kind, for today we were compatriot witnesses and both fearful of what was to come.

While we waited for Brad Hall, a reporter approached us. We chatted about the case and why we were there. When he asked our names Steel became agitated, insisting that the reporter not print his name. Was he still hung up on his given name, Byron? I wondered if he'd done what he'd been threatening to do…officially change it. I didn't get a chance to ask him, as our conversation was interrupted by the arrival of Brad.

In the courthouse we were ushered into the witnesses' room to wait our turn to be called into court. This small room was akin to an unwelcoming doctor's waiting room. No window, nothing to read and a variety of uncomfortable chairs lined against the walls. Brad introduced us to the other expert witnesses and the police officers and we took a seat. We sat in silence, stared into space or read our statements again, everyone in their own world. My attempts at conversation were not fruitful.

'Gee, it's cold today', was met with weak smiles and nodding heads that quickly bent back to re-read their statements.

'The accident on Bruce Highway was nasty, wasn't it?' received more nods. Aside from picking my nails, shivering and sighing, there was little to do but sit and observe my room mates. My 20-odd page statement was firmly embedded in my psyche and it beat me how the guy sitting next to me could still be reading his half-page statement after half an hour.

'How long are we going to be in here?' I asked.

'As long as it takes; could be all day', answered one of the detectives.

'What order do we go into court?' I questioned, in the hope that an escape to a warm coffee shop might be possible.

'You're probably last of this lot and before me', Brad offered.

There were at least five people in front of me. I could escape.

'Anyone for a sausage roll and hot chocolate?' I chirped. It worked. Three of us took orders and dashed across the street. The smell of warm pastries and hot drinks lifted the tone of the room.

Our numbers dwindled quickly as the first few witnesses each went in and came out after 10 to 15 minutes. Steel was called in halfway through the morning, leaving only me, Brad and another officer in the room. This suited me fine, for I felt more comfortable expressing my fears to Brad and asking his advice in the absence of more experienced expert witnesses. He assured me that there was nothing to worry about and that my evidence was just 'the icing on the cake'.

Twenty minutes later, Steel bounced out of the courtroom in typical Sammy Steel style, bubbling with enthusiasm and sporting a wide grin. It was a breeze. The only hard bit was spelling the names of the wattle species. Before he could say any more Brad cautioned him that he wasn't to share what had happened in the courtroom with us until we had each had our turn in the witness box.

I was glad Sammy had the spelling quiz, not me, and knew he would've been questioned on the botanical side of the case. I'd read part of his statement when we were sorting out the dates in Scientific Section. His part of the story ended where mine started. He detailed his search for pollen on tape-lifts from the defendant's clothing, his vegetation survey of Gympie, and the identification of the Noosa and Gympie wattle species. He also provided the botanical evidence such as the known distribution of the wattle species relevant to the case, the months in which they flowered and the limited dispersal of wattle pollen. From the latter he concluded that the likely source of wattle pollen on the defendant's clothing was from contact with flowering wattle plants. Steel's PhD research had shown wattle pollen had a limited dispersal; that sometimes it wasn't even represented in soil near a wattle plant; and that a very low percentage of wattle pollen was captured in pollen traps within 2 metres of a stand of wattle shrubs. This limited dispersal of wattle pollen had also been used as evidence in the New Zealand deer velvet case.[19]

After Steel's evidence all I needed to do was explain what species of wattle the pollen on the defendant's clothing and in the victim's car came from, and how I arrived at these conclusions. Simple, straightforward palynology.

Heartened by Steel's cheerful report that his courtroom experience hadn't been as traumatic as he'd expected, I relaxed back into my seat. But not for long. Paul Zohn emerged from the courtroom door and beckoned me in. It was my turn to leave the comfort of this now familiar room. With a deep breath and Brad's words that my evidence was just 'the icing on the cake' echoing in my mind, I followed Paul into the courtroom. Twenty minutes and I'd be out of there. Respectfully acknowledging the magistrate, as advised, I walked shakily to the raised witness box on the left-hand side of the room. After swearing that I would tell the truth, a young man rose from a table in the middle of the room and to my right. This must be the police prosecutor. He would lead me step by step through my evidence and highlight those parts he considered important.

Before a trial the prosecutor and an expert witness usually have a pre-trial conference to discuss the witness's evidence. This is for the prosecutor to learn from the witness the important aspects of their evidence and how best to present it, and for the witness to learn how their evidence fits into the general 'case theory'. I had requested a conference with the prosecutor prior to the committal, but it wasn't deemed necessary. He would only ask me questions he knew the answers to. I hoped this young prosecutor had read my statement thoroughly enough to ask the right questions. My role was to present the scientific evidence without bias, but if the right questions weren't asked of me, I'd be defenceless during the cross-examination. This was my greatest fear.

While the prosecutor shuffled his papers I glanced around the room. Behind the bench at which the prosecutor and defence counsel sat was the public seating, and to my left, the District Magistrate sat behind a raised desk—nothing I hadn't expected. Directly in front of me and on the other side of the courtroom was a glass partition behind which a man lounged insolently in his chair, eyeing me with disdain. This must be the defendant. If his demeanour was designed to 'freak out the witness' he was doing a good job.

The prosecutor led me through stating my name, occupation and qualifications, and how my work experience was relevant to the case, before drawing from me my 'evidence-in-chief', as it is called. Thankfully he'd prepared well, understood my statement and did most of the talking. I was not the most coherent of witnesses but considering the defendant's campaign to unnerve me and it being my first time as an expert witness, I was not too distressed. But so much for 20 minutes. It was an hour before the prosecutor finished with me and we adjourned for lunch.

Brad Hall, Steel, another police officer and I went to the RSL club for lunch. Apprehensive about my cross-examination after lunch, I asked Steel what his cross-examination had been like. Before he could answer, Brad interrupted, again cautioning us that we were not allowed to discuss this.

Foiled, but still wanting to know what to expect, when we returned to the courthouse I looked for someone who might be able to help me. A friendly female reporter from the local newspaper obliged.

'What is the defence lawyer like?' I asked.

'He's a nice enough guy, but he won't necessarily be nice when he's questioning you', she answered.

'What kind of things will he do?' I queried apprehensively.

'He can be rude and aggressive and will try to attack your credibility', she explained.

My oh my, was I an innocent. 'How do other witnesses deal with that?' I asked, desperately hoping that the door to the courtroom wouldn't open and beckon me in before my new-found mentor could answer.

'The most important thing is not to take it personally', she advised. 'Don't get defensive and angry, even if he does rattle you. If you get angry, it will destroy your credibility and the magistrate may think you're not impartial.'

'Heavens. I'm not good at taking a barrage of criticism and not reacting', I admitted ruefully. Answering back at school and passionately defending myself and others who had been wronged got me into hot water frequently.

'Take your time to answer the questions. If you don't know the answer, say so', she advised. 'If he asks you something that isn't in your field of expertise, say "That is outside my field of expertise". You should address that to the magistrate. Don't forget to call him Your Worship when you address him', she cautioned.

'I have to call him Your Worship, not Your Honour?' I asked.

'Yes, Your Honour is how you address judges', she explained.

Wow, why didn't I find this lady before? She was a mine of information. Before I could learn more, Paul called me into the courtroom.

It was ten minutes before the magistrate graced us with his presence. The prosecutor and defence counsel joked and laughed together. Kindly they asked if I would like a glass of water. I did, and it was promptly supplied. This was all very friendly and I relaxed. Surely that nice man wasn't going to be rude to me? The defendant also seemed in better humour after lunch. He was leaning on the desk in front of him and keenly watching the friendly exchange in the courtroom.

The magistrate finally came into the courtroom and we all rose. Before he began his cross-examination the defence counsel smiled sweetly at me and I back at him. Did I detect a hint of the curled lip of a dog about to attack its victim in that smile? A chill went through me and the friendly atmosphere in the room vanished. I was dinner, and I steeled myself for what was to come.

First the defence counsel established how the pollen samples were treated, then he tried to make me admit that the chemicals used would markedly alter the appearance of pollen grains. Of course, they don't. Silly man. Then came the wind theory. How many tests, if any, had I done to show how far wattle pollen could travel on a windy and rainy day?...None personally, but colleagues had. Sensing my inexperience in a courtroom, he honed in on other opinions I held that relied on someone else's work, implying that I wasn't an expert in my area.

'What other aspects of this statement are hearsay? What else were you *told*?' he raged, slamming my statement down onto the table in disgust. I quivered, and there began my decline. Anger wasn't far away. The prosecutor could have objected to this question but he didn't, perhaps because this was only a committal. I now know that expert witnesses can use hearsay—information based on their peers' research.

Further questions were asked of me that seemed ridiculous to a palynologist, but would appear feasible to a lay person. My role was to answer the questions, not give a lesson in palynology, and this I found frustrating. Each time my words were turned against me, I became more defensive, angry and closer to tears. I was doing exactly what I'd been advised not to do.

The time it took to roll out a TV set for me to watch a video of the Noosa crime scene provided a welcome chance to gather my thoughts and control my emotions. Scrutinising my fingernails below the bench of the witness box I tried to block out the environment and pull myself together. This was a nasty game and I didn't want to play any more. I didn't have to take this shit but the only person who could help me was me. I could do it. This resolved, I straightened my back and prepared to watch the video.

As the vegetation at the crime scene panned across the screen I was questioned about the plant types present. I'm a geologist and have no trouble naming pollen, but identifying their parent plants at that time was beyond me. Struggling to remember the phrase the reporter said I should use in situations like this I uttered 'I'm not a botanist' or 'I wasn't asked to examine that' and finally I got it right: 'That is outside my field of expertise'. In the end it was not so hard after all, as long as I kept my cool.

It took the defence counsel an hour to chew me up and spit me out. Shakily I left the witness box, eyes firmly focussed on the floor, embarrassed and ashamed of my lack of control in the middle of the cross-examination. Tripping over my feet would be the penultimate humiliation and, if my eyes met with pitying ones from the public stalls, I would burst into tears. Paul Zohn met me at the rear of the courtroom and put his arm around my shoulder as he led me out the door.

'You did good, mate, honest', he reassured me. I didn't believe him but was pleased he recognised that I needed supportive words. Reading through the transcripts of my cross-examination years later, it was apparent that I was nervous but what I said made sense to me. My embarrassment has long gone and I'm now much wiser. It was a lesson I had to have.

Steel and Brad Hall were waiting in the foyer when I emerged from the courtroom, shattered. So much for Brad's comment about 'icing on the cake'. Or was he right? My interpretation of his comment was that my evidence was incidental. The witnesses before me were providing the basic ingredients and cooking the cake. I was to provide the decoration—a simple sweetener on top of the cake. But instead of a simple cake it had been an intricately decorated cake with icing that could crumble if it was applied by a novice.

I needed a drink, or two, to debrief. I felt violated. It was a week before this feeling disappeared, and only after a friend who had spent 20 minutes in a witness box several weeks beforehand confessed that he also had felt the same and for as long, did I begin to recover my poise.

Steel and I waited with Brad Hall in the courthouse foyer while two other police officers gave their evidence. By late afternoon we were in the RSL club hoping the magistrate would make his decision before we left and while we were still sober. Sitting on high stools around a free-standing bench and with a refreshing beer in our hands, we each chose a number and contributed one dollar to a game of keno. While sharing out our winnings half an hour later, the news came over from the courthouse that the magistrate had made his decision. The case was to be committed to trial. The prosecution's evidence had been sufficiently solid to warrant a trial.

In early 1998 my daughters, the dog and I left Brisbane to return to Perth. We drove overland to Adelaide, then flew the last leg of the trip. At the last minute I packed up the boxes of my thesis material that I'd originally intended to leave at a friend's place until I returned for the trial, and posted them to Perth. A fortunate decision.

Shortly before the trial, and as I was expecting my plane ticket from Perth to Brisbane to arrive, Paul Zohn phoned me to say that the prosecutor had discussed the pollen evidence with Steel and had decided not to use it in the trial. Because the trial was only days away this decision apparently couldn't be changed. I was shocked, disappointed and angry beyond belief. Paul was unhappy and baffled by this turn of events and so were Alan Bourke and the victim's family—without the pollen evidence there was a chance that Holden could be found not guilty of murder.

It transpired that the defence were considering employing a colleague of mine who they hoped would suggest that prevailing winds and rain could have carried wattle pollen from Noosa to Gympie. Aside from an emphatic 'Bullshit!', my answer to this is unprintable. Of course, there are always exceptions to rules, but in the context of the number of wattle pollen grains present on Holden's clothing and in the victim's car relative to the other pollen types present, I doubt the defence's counter to this evidence would've been sustained. Since then I have heard that the defence believed the pollen evidence was based on only one pollen grain. This wasn't the case. Even if it was, it was irrelevant when placed in context. After all, wasn't a single fossil pollen grain the grain of truth in a 1960 murder case in Austria?

During the following weeks I worried about what the outcome of the trial might be—would a murderer walk free?—and wondered what had transpired to make Steel cease to support the pollen evidence. This evidence was my field and my responsibility, not Steel's. His evidence related to the botanical survey of Gympie and initial scanning of the tape-lift slides. So why didn't the prosecutor ask my opinion? No doubt he knew what he was doing. In retrospect, and now somewhat wiser in the ways of the law and forensic science, I respect his decision. As for Steel, his own research about the dispersal of wattle pollen supported the pollen evidence, so I wondered why he didn't push for it to be used. I've had no contact with him since the committal. I know he did finish his PhD and I believe he later completed another degree in a healing profession for which his effervescent personality would be well suited.

Several weeks after Paul's phone call, I received in the mail a photocopy of a newspaper article titled 'Pollen Traps Killer', sent to me by a dear friend, my former PhD supervisor. I was elated. Reas Holden had been convicted of Samantha Hall's murder and this article was a measure of the investigating team's belief that pollen had been the 'witness'. It provided the evidence for the police to arrest Holden, and later, when he pleaded not guilty at the committal, it played a major role in committing him to trial.

The journalist who wrote the article was given my Brisbane phone number by mistake and couldn't contact me, so my name wasn't mentioned. This was of little consequence. I'd been credited with having done the palynology on the case in an earlier newspaper article. The journalist eventually contacted Dr Dallas Mildenhall in New Zealand, who provided a better and more learned summary of forensic palynology in the article than I could have done at that time.

Some of what happened at the trial has since been related to me by the victim's family. They have told me that in the end the prosecution's case, which hung predominantly on the defendant's original confession and proven lies, was boosted by the defendant himself. He took the witness stand against his counsel's advice and called the police liars. The victim's family believe that this confirmed to those who made the judgement that it was he who was the liar.

In summing up at the end of the trial the judge told the defendant that he was a proven pathological liar and that he was despicable for putting the victim's family through this again (i.e. the committal and trial after first confessing). Reas Holden was found guilty of murder and sentenced to 25 years' imprisonment. He was arrested by pollen grains and convicted by his own confession and lies.

Epilogue

The new mother methodically chewed on the afterbirth, keeping a watchful eye on her newborn testing its unsteady legs. We stood apart, speaking in low tones so as not to disturb her maternal chore. Goose bumps on my arms testified to the chill in the air that accompanies the late winter dusk in southern Queensland. Chills ran through my body but they had little to do with the temperature. These ripples started at the base of my skull, encompassed it, then surged through my body in waves. To me they signified a truth, a moving revelation, a profound moment.

The bovine nativity was moving in itself, but it was not the cause of the ripples coursing through my body. Beside me, watching the new mother, stood a woman sharing with me the joys and sadness of her own motherhood. We had much in common, yet we were worlds apart. In common we loved our children with a passion and hugged them often; our shared philosophy of life enabled us to face adversity with courage and humour and rise from the ashes stronger; and we shared a frankness of expression that often belied our femininity. We were like minds, but we differed in the intensity of our life experiences. She had survived something more devastating than I could imagine. The murder of her younger daughter.

As she spoke I marvelled at her courage and frankness and was drawn to share the emotion behind the words—wishing I could take some of the load from her and at the same time trying to fathom the burden itself. How would I feel in the same situation? Devastated. Impotent. Robbed. Vengeful. Fleetingly, words of this ilk flashed through my mind. I looked into the depth beyond her eyes, into the pain she had endured and still carried with her. I stood in awe of this remarkable woman, oblivious to the cold and my numb bare arms.

It was almost dark. Only a vestige of the twilight remained. She called to her husband—a man who shared her burden with an open gentleness and passion that belied his generation—patiently standing by the four-legged mother.

'It's getting cold and dark. Surely we can bring her in now?' she implored.

He nodded, and began to usher the cow and its newborn calf towards the gate and the safety of the night yard. We ambled beside them, still talking.

'You know, there's one thing that I'll forever be thankful for', she said, lifting her eyes from the ground and turning toward me.

'It's the hugs and cuddles. I have those to remember', she said.

The chills rippled through my body again, wave after wave. My arrival some half an hour beforehand came back to mind. The urge to hug her the moment I saw her was so strong that nothing could have stopped me. As we hugged I knew that whatever had compelled me to drive from Noosa to Gympie that afternoon had reached its destination.

We spent the evening around their kitchen table eating home-made chips and home-grown ham and eggs, washed down by a bottle of wine and home-brewed Midori. Their home was full of warmth, love, banter, laughter and the cutest tiny dogs I had ever seen. I fell in love. Her name was Pippy. She snuggled contentedly into the crook of my neck providing a welcome comfort as I vicariously lived through the story that unfolded. I listened, disturbed by the brazenness of their daughter's killer and moved beyond words by the repercussions of his actions. Here was a family that had been put through unimaginable horror and stress. Here were two children left motherless and with a father they may never wish to know. And here, too, were the retired grandparents who fought for and won custody of their daughter's children. The emotional toll for them will be forever.

The sadness, anger and grief these amazing people shared with me was peppered with tales of love and laughter. We also discussed the blight of domestic violence and homicide: how some men's ultimate act of control leads to a woman's death; how their victims feel worthless and know that one day they will be killed. We spoke of their desire to escape their captors and raise their children in a happy home. As I sat in this small cosy farmhouse amid renovations that had all but come to a halt since two small children moved in, I realised that the children's mother had made the ultimate sacrifice. What better place for her children to be raised?

It was not long off midnight. Time had flown. Thoughts of how I would get back to Noosa in a Midori haze without getting lost hadn't crossed my mind.

But it did my hosts'. We left shortly before midnight. They drove in front of me for half an hour, guiding me through the maze of country roads that was the short way to Noosa. Malcolm stopped at the main road, got out and walked back to give me a hug and extract a promise to phone them the moment I arrived at the hotel in Noosa. I did. My eyes filled with tears as I put the phone down. I missed them already. In the fog that filled my head it dawned on me that this was not an ending; it was a beginning.

Researching and writing this book has been a physical, emotional and enlightening journey that I have had the honour of sharing with two very special people—Lyn and Malcolm Hall, Samantha Hall's courageous parents who have raised her two small boys to fine young teenagers. It has in turn been a humbling and uplifting experience. In a letter to me Lyn wrote that she hoped the experience would not damage me. I was humbled by her concern after all that she had endured, and assured her that although it might change me, it was an experience I had to have. The uplifting side has been our friendship, the laughter, shared intimacies and the knowledge that forensic palynology made a difference in their lives.

During the evening we spent together and subsequent long phone calls, these wonderful people have shared with me Samantha's story and shown me what lies behind the scenes of domestic violence and homicide. They introduced me to the Sam they knew and loved, filled the gaps in my knowledge of the case, and convincingly illustrated why they believe their daughter's murder was carefully planned. The latter had crossed my mind as I drove along the road from Noosa to Gympie. Even with the little I knew at that time it seemed too neat, too trite a scenario, for it to be an accidental crime of passion. Later, with more knowledge of events, the web woven to provide windows of opportunity and alibis became blatantly clear.

Some of the web is still missing—but there are clues I hope to follow up one day. Depressions in Samantha's skull were consistent with those caused by a heavy implement. Where is the baseball bat that was kept in the convicted person's car? And where are the shoes he wore on the night of the murder? The unidentified wattle pollen on his clothing and in the victim's car may provide the answer.

In his original confession Samantha Hall's former partner admitted that he had killed her, but in a fit of rage. The statement also contained apologies to his and Samantha's family but, tellingly, he followed this with an assertion that what he did was 'something he had to do'.

My meeting with Lyn and Malcolm Hall was unplanned but, I believe, meant to be. It convinced me that I was meant to tell Samantha's story alongside the story of forensic palynology and my experiences in it. Lyn and Malcolm gave me their blessing to do so—not only for Sam, but in the hope that it will raise awareness of domestic homicide and its repercussions. They share with me a conviction that society should provide assistance for men who breach restraining orders—perhaps counselling in a compulsory residential environment; and that more realistic compensation should be available for the living victims of domestic homicide.

Unacknowledged victims themselves, Lyn and Malcolm fought for their grandchildren to be recognised as victims of crime. The children received a token amount through their efforts. In the time that this couple should be enjoying their retirement, they are lovingly struggling to provide for their unexpected second family. The fruits of their labours are evident in the cheeky grins of their grandchildren. But as for all unsung victims of domestic violence and homicide, the consequences and emotional toll left by this insidious crime will not go away. They will stay with them, and their family and friends, for life.

Glossary and Abbreviations

CIB Crime Investigation Branch
CMM Centre for Microscopy and Microanalysis.
DNA Deoxyribonucleic acid. The substance that genes are made of and that determines the inherited characteristics of living organisms.
DSS Detective Senior Sergeant.
HCl Hydrochloric acid.
HF Hydrofluoric acid.
KOH Potassium hydroxide.
RSL Returned Services League.
SEM Scanning Electron Microscopy.
TEM Transmission Electron Microscopy.
μm Micrometre. A metric unit. There are 1000 μm in 1 centimetre.

acetolysis A chemical technique used to remove the inner contents and the lipids on the outside of pollen and spores in order to clearly see their structure in light *microscopy*.
assemblage (i.e. 'pollen assemblage') All the pollen and spore types found together in a single sample.
biopolymer Polymers are many small molecules of the same kind bonded to form a larger molecule. Biopolymers are naturally occurring polymers, e.g. starch, cellulose, protein, rubber. The walls of most pollen and spores predominantly consist of a biopolymer called sporopollenin.
cannabis Marijuana.
chemiluminescence A chemical reaction that produces light.
cleistogamous Plants that pollinate themselves without the flowers ever having to open; also called 'closed pollination'. The most common plants that use closed pollination are cereals.
committal A hearing before a magistrate to determine if there is enough evidence to commit a person suspected of a crime to trial.
compound microscope A microscope that uses more than one lens in sequence to increase the degree of magnification.

complainant A person who brings a charge against another person to court; normally a police officer in the case of minor offences and the State for serious offences.

control sample A sample taken from the scene of a crime, or other areas of interest, to provide a baseline for comparison with samples collected from suspects, victims or items of interest.

cytoplasm All the internal contents of a cell excluding the nucleus.

defence counsel The lawyer acting for the accused person.

defendant A person accused of committing a crime.

dinoflagellates Microscopic aquatic organisms variously considered to be algae, protozoans or protists that are abundant in plankton. Most are unicellular, flagellate and marine, but they also occur in fresh water and even snow.

electron microscope A microscope that uses an electron beam and electromagnetic lenses instead of a light beam and glass lenses; has greater resolving and magnifying powers than a light microscope.

entomologist A person who studies insects.

evidence tape Special tape that is placed across the seal of *exhibit* bags (or boxes and vials) that police use to carry items that may contain evidence in a criminal case; the tape is signed by the person who last sealed the bag.

exhibits In a police context, any items that may contain evidence of a criminal act (e.g. clothing, guns, rope, vehicles).

expert witness A person who provides an opinion in court based on their expertise in a field of study in which jurors are unlikely to be knowledgeable.

focus wheel A small wheel on a microscope that, when turned, adjusts the focus level on the object being viewed.

footlayer The inner (third) layer of a pollen wall that supports the *infratectum* and *tectum*.

forensic Pertaining to techniques used to analyse evidence used in courts of law.

forensic sample In a palynological context, a sample from an item or person of interest in a criminal case that may contain evidence to support or discount a connection between that item or person and the crime.

granulate A term used to describe the type of pollen surface sculpture that consists of very small (less than 1 μm) rounded elements.

heavy liquid A chemical solution that is heavier than water (e.g. zinc bromide).

herbarium (pl. herbaria) A collection of dried and pressed plant specimens mounted on cardboard; may be a personal collection or a large State-funded collection. Specimens are labelled with the plant name, where and when they were collected and by whom.

homicide The killing of a human being.
infratectum The pollen wall layer (second) between the *tectum* and *footlayer*; sometimes called the columellate layer.
jurisdiction The area or territory over which laws or other State powers are extended.
lipids A term used here to describe the sticky material often found covering the outer layer of the pollen wall.
littoral The beach environment between the highest and lowest tide levels.
macrofossils Fossil plant or animal remains large enough to be seen with the naked eye.
microfossils Fossil plant or animal remains that can only be seen with the aid of a microscope.
micrometre (μm) A metric unit; there are 1000 μm in 1 centimetre.
micropalaeontology The study of microscopic fossil animal (and some plant) remains that are not resistant to the acids used for palynology preparations.
microscopy The use of a microscope.
monad An individual pollen grain.
morphology The study of the structure and form of organisms.
palaeopalynology The study of fossil pollen, spores and other *palynomorphs* found in sediments older than 2 million years.
palynology The study of fossil or modern pollen, spores and/or other *palynomorphs*.
palynologist A person who practises *palynology*.
palynomorph A general term for all microscopic particles (e.g. pollen, spores, dinoflagellates, freshwater algal cysts) studied by palynologists.
palynostratigraphy The use of *palynomorphs* to determine the relative age of, and relationship between, different rock layers (strata).
pathologist A person who studies diseased or damaged tissues.
pipette A glass tube with a rubber bulb attached to one end (or a plastic tube sealed at one end); used to transfer liquids from one container to another.
polyad More than four individual pollen grains (*monads*) dispersed together as a single unit.
prosecutor Lawyer who acts on behalf of the *complainant* in a criminal case.
Quaternary palynology The study of pollen and spores found in sediments that are no older than 2 million years.
radiocarbon dating (carbon-14 or 14^{C}) A method of dating that uses the rate of decay of the radioactive element carbon-14; only useful for rocks/objects no older than about 70000 years.

rhinitis Inflammation of nasal tissues.

sedimentology The study of sediments (water-deposited particles).

sculpture (i.e. pollen wall sculpture) Patterns on the outer layer of the pollen wall.

strata Layers.

stub In the context of electron microscopy, a metal button on which the specimen to be examined in an *SEM* microscope is secured.

supernatant Predominantly liquid part of a suspension that floats above the more solid parts that settle out of the suspension after it has been left to stand for some time, or after it has been centrifuged.

tape-lift Adhesive tape that has been pressed against an object to collect dust particles and fibres.

tectal island Here used to describe a discrete raised area of *tectum* on the surface of a pollen grain.

tectum The outer layer of the pollen wall.

transmitted light microscope A microscope that uses a beam of light that passes through the medium or substrate in which the object being viewed is held, as opposed to a microscope that uses light reflected from the object.

traveller wheel Used here to describe the small wheel on a microscope that, when moved, moves the microscope slide along and up and down so that different parts of the slide can be viewed.

water mount Used here to describe pollen temporarily mounted on a microscope slide in water, as opposed to pollen permanently mounted in a plastic or other mounting medium.

References

1 Locard, E., 1928, 'Dust and its analysis', 1. *Police Journal*, 177.

2 Wodehouse, R. P., 1935, *Pollen Grains*, McGraw-Hill, New York.

3 Maslin, B. R., 2001, 'Introduction', *Acacia, Flora of Australia* 11A, pp. 3–13.

4 Mabberley, D. J., 1997, *The Plant Book. A Portable Dictionary of the Vascular Plants*, Cambridge University Press, UK.

5 Wattle Day, 2002, http://farrer.riv.csu.edu.au/ASGAP/wattle_d.html

6 Hyde, H. A. and Williams, D. A., 1944, 'The right word', *Pollen Analysis Circular*, 8, p. 6.

7 Jansonius, J. and McGregor, D. C., 1996, 'Introduction', in *Palynology: Principles and Applications*, J. Jansonius and D. C. McGregor (eds), vol. 1, pp. 1–10. American Association of Stratigraphic Palynologists Foundation.

8 Press, F. and Siever, R., 1974, *Earth*, W. H. Freeman and Company, San Francisco.

9 Lampe, D., 1990, 'Reader of the invisible dust', *The World and I*, 15 (11), pp. 316–323.

10 Leroi-Gourhan, A., 1975, 'The flowers found with Shanidar IV, a Neanderthal burial in Iraq', *Science*, 190, pp. 562–564.

11 Stanley, E. A., 1992, 'Application of palynology to establish the provenance and travel history of illicit drugs', *Microscope* 40, pp. 149–152.

12 Erdtman, G., 1969, *Handbook of Palynology*, Hafner, New York.

13 Mildenhall, D. C., 1998, 'A grain of evidence: Invisible pollen grains can be enough to sort out the guilty and the innocent', *New Zealand Science Monthly*, June.

14 Mildenhall, D. C., 1982, 'Forensic palynology', *Geological Society of New Zealand Newsletter* 58, p. 25.

15 Mildenhall, D. C. 1990, 'Forensic palynology in New Zealand', *Review of Palaeobotany and Palynology* 64–65, pp. 227–234.

16 Bryant, V. M. Jr and Mildenhall, D. C., 1998, 'Forensic palynology: A new way to catch crooks', in *New Developments in Palynomorph Sampling, Extraction, and Analysis*, V. M. Bryant and J. W. Wrenn (eds), American Association of Stratigraphic Palynologists Foundation, Contribution Series No. 33, pp. 145–155.

17 Palenik, S., 1982, 'Microscopic trace evidence—the overlooked clue: Part II, Max Frei—Sherlock Holmes with a microscope', *Microscope* 30, pp. 163–168.

18 Danin, A, and Baruch, U., 2001, 'Floristic indicators for the origin of the Shroud of Turin', in *The Shroud of Turin: Unravelling the mystery*, A. D. Adler, I. Piczek, and M. Minor (eds), Proceedings of the 1998 Dallas Symposium, Alexander Books, Alexander, North Carolina, pp. 202–214.

19 Mildenhall, D. C., 1988, 'Deer velvet and palynology: An example of the use of forensic palynology in New Zealand', *Tuatara*, 30 (1), pp. 1–11.